Langu

Richard Sale

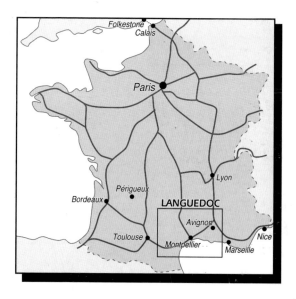

A research scientist before concentrating on travel
writing and photography, Richard's titles for Landmark
include the Côte d'Azur, Cotswolds, Dartmoor, Dorset,
Italian Lakes, Madeira, Provence and Somerset.

AVEYRON

Rodez

3 Mende

ARDÈCHE

2 LOZÈRE

Alès   Orange

Millau   GARD

Albi

AVIGNON

1

TARN   HÉRAULT

NÎMES

Castries   Arle

MONTPELLIER

4

Canal du Midi   Béziers

CARCASSONNE   Narbonne

AUDE

N
W   E
S

0   15miles
0   20kms

PERPIGNAN

LANGUEDOC

PYRÉNÉES-
ORIENTALES

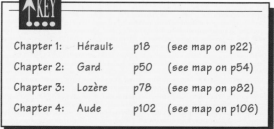

Languedoc

Richard Sale

Introduction

Languedoc is the forgotten – or should that be undiscovered – south of France. For many visitors southern France is Provence and the Côte d'Azur. The Autoroute du Soleil (the A7) splits at Orange, the A8 traversing Provence on its way to the Côte d'Azur and the Italian border: that is the way most of the traffic goes.

But visitors who follow the A9, head westwards into Gard, one of the four Languedocian *départements*. Within these *départements* there is a sample, at the very least, of everything that France has to offer. Scenically the area is magnificent, varying from the high, wooded hills of the Cévennes National Park, to the beautiful farmland of the coastal plain and the extraordinary limestone plateaux of the Causses. Historically, Languedoc is fascinating, the medieval city of Carcassone being as definitively European as the Renaissance cities of Italy, the Cathar castles being at once architecturally splendid and crucial to the development of France. Nîmes has some of the best preserved

Roman monuments in any part of the old Empire, while Montpellier is a thriving, bustling modern city. Then there is the coast, less exploited than that of the Côte d'Azur, but no less worthwhile, its beaches as good.

The result of the interplay of geography and history in the area covered by the book is to have created a region tailor-made for the visitor – there is always something interesting around the next corner. And as an added bonus, the crowds that sometimes make visits to the sights of Provence difficult for the motorist are absent. In an area where space is one of the attractions, there is also space to enjoy it.

The geographical diversity and historical background of the region means that it is best to look separately at each of the *départements* that make it up rather than trying to divide it along other, more arbitrary, lines. Chapters are therefore devoted to Lozère, Gard, Hérault and Aude.

HISTORY

PRE-HISTORIC FRANCE

Early man crossed between Africa and Europe over the land bridge that existed, until fairly recent (on the time-scale of man's history) times, across the Straits of Gibraltar. Of these earliest men few traces remain, it being many thousands of years before man had evolved to the point where he could leave a tangible sign of his presence. At Lascaux, to the north of Languedoc, are the best known of these early signs, the cave paintings there being some of the earliest – and, remarkably, some of the finest – art

to have been created by our ancestors. The paintings date from about 25,000 years ago, the time of Palaeolithic (Old Stone Age) man.

For the non-expert, it is necessary to move forward perhaps 20,000 years before man's presence in the area becomes apparent. During the Neolithic (New Stone Age) period man began to use massive stones for ritual purposes and to mark the tombs of the dead. This is the time of the megalithic culture, dating originally to about 6,000 years ago, but lasting for many centuries. Although the region has nothing to compare with the extraordinary sites of Brittany, the dolmen (burial chambers – the eroded remains of long barrows) of Languedoc are recognized as being of a particular form and are of interest for that reason. The best of the sites are to be found in the Minervois district of Hérault.

GREEKS AND ROMANS

Neolithic man was replaced by Bronze Age folk, though many experts believe the transition was very gradual, metal users and stone users co-existing at first. Certainly the megalithic culture was still flourishing during the transition, the Languedoc dolmen being raised during the period now known as the Copper Age. Around 600BC two groups of invaders arrived in the region. By sea came the Phoenicians, who built a port at Agde as a trading and restocking post, while by land from central Europe came the iron-using Celts. The Phoenician, then Greek, settlers set up several ports along the coast, most notably at Marseille, while the less sophisticated Celts created their *oppida*, fortified hill villages.

It was these Celtic tribes who let

Hannibal pass unhindered in 218 BC when he crossed the Pyrénées into what is now Roussillon on his way to the Alps and Rome. That act was unlikely to have endeared the Celts of Languedoc to the Romans, though the invasion of the second century BC concerned empire-building rather than retribution. The Romans created splendid cities in Gaul (as they called Celtic France), the remains at Nîmes – the Arena and the Maison Carrée, a temple – being among the finest anywhere, while the aqueduct of Pont du Gard is still admired by architects and engineers alike. The Roman Via Domitia, which ran past Nîmes, followed a course now taken by the A9 autoroute, the name La Languedocienne for the road being supplemented along its length by silhouettes of a chariot, its driver's cloak flowing out behind him.

Via Domitia was heading for Narbo, now Narbonne, which gave its name to the Roman province of Narbonensis. When this province was split into two, for administrative reasons, the boundary was taken as the Rhône. This division was to have important repercussions centuries later when the kingdom of France, which had claimed western Narbonensis, stared across the Rhône at the lands of the Holy Roman Empire who sat in eastern Narbonensis. At Villenueve-les-Avignon and Beaucaire, medieval forts that defended this border can still be seen.

CHARLEMAGNE

When the Romans withdrew, the region was prey to barbarian invaders, Languedoc being taken by the Visigoths (from the east) and then the Saracens (invading westward from Spain). The Franks, who had invaded northern and central France in the fifth century as a number of isolated groups, were united under Clovis in the early sixth century. Clovis, one of history's more unpleasant characters, founded the Merovingian dynasty and gradually expanded his lands southward.

In 732 the Franks under Charles Martel won a decisive battle over the Saracens at Poitiers, though it was a further 200 years before the final Saracen enclave near Montpellier was destroyed. Though Charles Martel was never king of the Merovingian lands, he was a king-maker, founding the Carolingian dynasty when his son, Pepin I, become king in 751. Under a succession of able kings, especially Charlemagne (768-814), Charles Martel's grandson, the Carolingian empire expanded and consolidated.

Charlemagne was one of the finest rulers of First Millennium Europe. A powerful, brave and sometimes cruel warrior, he also had the tact and foresight to incorporate conquered peoples into the Carolingian empire rather than subject them to tyranny and, therefore, leave himself vulnerable to uprisings. However, ninth-century Europe was a time when princes ruled as much by strength of personality as strength of arm, and despite the groundwork of Charlemagne the empire eventually fell apart.

By the time Hugh Capet – his second name deriving from his liking for a short cape – ascended the throne in 987, France had fragmented, so that while he was nominally sovereign of the whole country, he was really only the ruler

Continued on page 12...

La gigude
Les embialades ←

Fromages de Chèvre

←

Above: Goat cheese sign, Aude

Right: Wine sign, Hérault

Below: Sunflower field, Aude

LES COTEAUX DES HAUTES GARRIGUES

Produits du Terroir

DEGUSTATION - VENTE

à 5 Km

Above: Dourbie Gorge
Below: Florac Château

of the north. In part this fragmentation was due to the lack of leaders of the quality of Charles Martel and Charlemagne. But in large part it was due to language differences between northern and southern France.

Langue d'Oc

Roman Gaul spoke Latin, but in the years after the Roman withdrawal the language became adulterated with the Germanic dialects of the Franks and Saxons and with words from older, Celtic, languages. Gradually two forms of Latin developed in France. To the north there was Langue d'Oïl, so called because the word for yes was oïl, while in the south there was Langue d'Oc, with yes rendered as oc. In time Langue d'Oïl become French, oïl becoming oui. The southern language gave its name to the region and become the language now known as Provençal or Occitan (though the latter is actually a concocted word with little genuine ancestry). An edict of 1539 made Langue d'Oïl the official language of France, though Langue d'Oc continued to be the first language of the south until it was banned in schools in the early nineteenth century. Only in 1951 was this ban revoked.

In 1854 Frédéric Mistral revived interest in the language by forming the Félibrige (from an old Oc word meaning 'doctor') dedicated to preserving it. Mistral was awarded the Nobel Prize for Literature in 1904, some of his epic poems being written in Provençal. Today the language clings on, somewhat precariously, though many of the inhabitants of Languedoc still have a smattering of the old words in their dialect.

THE ALBEGENSIAN CRUSADE

After William of Normandy claimed the English throne in 1066 the kings of France – the Capetian dynasty, named after Hugh Capet – were too occupied with resisting an English take over of northern France to be bothered with the southerners: they spoke a different language and were a long way off.

However by the start of the thirteenth century things had changed. The south, to the west of the Rhône had been divided by the counts of Barcelona and Toulouse. Languedoc became the province of the Count of Toulouse, with Roussillon going to the Count of Barcelona. When the King of Aragon took over the Barcelonan lands, Roussillon brought the border of this powerful kingdom to the northern side of the Pyrénées. At the same time there were suspicions that Aragon was negotiating a treaty with the Count of Toulouse. If Languedoc fell, then Aragon would include southern France as far as the Rhône.

Providentially, for the king of France that is, the concerns over Aragon and Languedoc coincided with the rise of Catharism. Catharism was based on the town of Albi – hence the occasional name of Albigenses, and the name of the Crusade against the Cathars – but enjoyed the support of the Count of Toulouse. In 1208 the Pope sent an envoy to the Count, Raymond VI, seeking permission to send

Catharism

Catharism is a cult whose origins are still disputed. Its believers held that two gods ruled creation, a good god who reigned over the spiritual realm of heaven and an evil god who reigned over all material worlds, including the earth. Some see elements of ancient Persian beliefs, even of Zoroastrianism and eastern mysticism in Catharism, but there was also a strong element of Christianity.

Cathars (the word derives from the Greek for 'pure') believed that Jesus Christ was a spiritual presence on earth (not a material form), sent to show the righteous path to heaven, and believed the Catholic church to be heretical. Cathars rejected Mass, the Old Testament, marriage, burial rituals, even organized religion, though they did have a priesthood. The priests, or parfaits (perfects ones) could be men or women. They wore simple clothes, were celibate, ate a simple diet and apart from the interpretation of the Gospels, existed chiefly to carry out the *consolamentum*, the Cathar baptism. Only after this baptism were Cathars required to forego the evil pleasures of the natural world as a preparation for death and heaven, so it was performed when the believer was dying.

Catholic missionaries to convert the Cathars. The envoy, Pierre de Castelnau, was murdered at St Gilles, near Nîmes.

Whether this was a fortunate co-incidence or an engineered situation is not known, but the French king used it as an excuse to start a Crusade against the Cathars. It began in 1209 and the Crusade, led by Simon de Montfort and Arnold Amaury, the Abbot of Cîteaux, lasted 20 bloody years, with tens of thousands of Languedocians, Cathars and Catholics alike, being slaughtered. In 1229 the Treaty of Meaux ended the Crusade, Languedoc becoming part of France, though some Cathars continued to resist. Not until 1255 did the last stronghold, the Château de Quéribus fall. Even then, it was another 100 years before Catharism finally died out.

THE WARS OF RELIGION

The castles in western Languedoc that were Cathar strongholds now became fortresses on the border with Aragon, though the French king was soon more troubled by the English, north across the Channel. The Hundred Years War ebbed and flowed around Languedoc as elsewhere, peace only arriving in the mid-fifteenth century.

In the stability of the next 100 years, resentment within Languedoc of the French-speaking, Catholic-dominated establishment in the north (who, they felt, only noticed them when it was time to collect taxes) grew. Protestantism was a natural choice for this anti-Catholic feeling, though the Huguenot uprisings were fuelled by the resentments of rural folk to their Parisian masters throughout France, and even by political intrigue (as the St Bartholomew's Day Massacre in Paris in 1572 shows). Ultimately there was civil war, with further killings in Languedoc in the name of religion. The Edict of Nantes in 1598 brought token peace and free-

Above: Florac

Left: Sports shop, L'Espérou

dom of religion, but within 100 years the Edict had been revoked and war began again. In 1622 Protestant Montpellier, a city seen, rightly, as supporting the new faith in order to confront the northern establishment, was besieged and almost destroyed.

In Languedoc, at the end of the seventeenth century the fighting was taken up by the Camisards. The name is disputed, some seeing it as deriving from the camisole-like smocks of the peasant guerrillas, some from the Provençal words for an 'attacker by night'. The Camisard war, begun by the killing of the Abbé Chayla at Le Pont-de-Montvert in July 1702, lasted for two years, ending with the executions of many Camisard leaders.

REVOLUTION AND MODERN FRANCE

The Revolution of 1789 united France in a way that no king ever quite managed. The Napoleonic era, and the industrialization that followed, cemented this union so that today Languedoc is as French as any region – though there are those that still hanker after the further revival of the Provençal language and the northern Languedocian villages are still the chief area of French Protestantism.

GEOGRAPHY

Around 600 million years ago, during the Primary Era of geological time, an earth movement known as the Hercynian Fold forced a vast, V-shaped mass of rock above the sea that covered what is now France. The arms of this V formed Brittany and the Ardennes, while at its base lay the Massif Central. To the south of the V lay Tyrrhenia, a land that later erosion and inundation would carve into Provence, the Balearic Islands, Corsica and Sardinia. During the Secondary Era of geological time sedimentary layers of rock were laid down below the clear waters of the sea that lay between the rock masses.

Then during the Tertiary Era (from about 65 million years ago until about 2 million years ago) plate tectonics created the young mountains of the Pyrénées and the Alps, while at the same time lifting the area that is now the south of France above the sea. The compressive pressures that raised the two mountain blocks caused molten magma to be forced upwards through fault lines, creating the volcanoes that are so prominent a feature of the northern Massif Central (whose inactive cones now form the Auvergne Volcano Park), and the outcrops of igneous rock to the north-east of Béziers.

In the north of the area covered by this book, the old rocks of the Massif Central still underlie the soil. This forms Haut Vivarais and the Cévennes, and, to the southwest, the Montage Noir and Minervois. Between these old rocks lie the sedimentary rocks laid down beneath the Secondary Era's sea, the limestones of the Bas Vivarais in Ardèche, the Grands Causses of northern Languedoc and the sedimentary strata of Bas Languedoc. Finally, the coastline is created from very new strata, the alluvial sediments of the Quaternary Era, the most recent era of geological time.

The geography of the region is so singular that a National Park (the Cévennes) and a Regional Park (the Haut Languedoc) have been created to protect areas of it. Add to those parks the limestone caves and gorges of the Causses and the Ardèche, and it can be seen that Languedoc has a multiplicity of natural wonders. The natural vegetation of the region's northern hills, where the rainfall is high due to the collision of water-ladened, cool Atlantic air and dry, warm Mediterranean air, is a thick forest of beech, chestnut and pine. Lower down, and closer to the coast, the forest is replaced by the *garrigue*, a thin, spiky mix of holm oak, broom, juniper and other hardy plants, interspersed with *maquis*, the typical southern France growth of aromatic herbs – mint, thyme, rosemary and lavender.

However, the rivers that drain winter's snows down to the sea create fertile valleys, despite the long hot summers, and their waters have also been used to irrigate the plains. On this fertile land grow cereals, sunflowers, orchards and, most particularly, vineyards. Sheep and cows are kept, particularly on the arid grasslands of the Causses, and the old ritual of the transhumance still transfers them from high (summer) to low (winter) pasture in autumn, and back again in spring.

The valleys of Languedoc grow a wide range of vegetables, while the plains support orchards, soft fruit and herbs. Add to this the fungi and chestnuts gathered from the hill woods and the possibilities for game in the same woods – wild boar (*sanglier*), hare, rabbit and pigeon, and it is no surprise to discover that the local cuisine is basic and earthy. To some that will seem a derogatory description: it is not. Rather, it is complimentary, the cuisine offering good ingredients prepared with a minimum of fuss, just right for appetites generated by walking, canoeing or the exertions of sightseeing.

Any discussion of Languedocian cuisine must start with *cassoulet*. This thick casserole consists of white beans, meat, sausage and goose fat, well seasoned with herbs. The 'real' *cassoulet* from Castelnaudary (the town claiming not only to be the birthplace of the dish but the only place where the authentic *cassoulet* can be enjoyed) is made with pork meat and is usually seasoned with garlic. However, good *cassoulet* can also be made with a mix of mutton and pork sausage. Connoisseurs treat this *cassoulet de Carcassonne* with disdain, but well-prepared it is just as good.

The game meats, not only wild animals and birds, but goat, are often served barbecued (*méchoui*). The very best barbecues use *sarments*, vine cuttings, to import a distinctive flavour, the meat being eaten with a plain salad and hunks of fresh bread.

In the hills of the Cévennes stews are popular – the right food for a man who has spent the day outside in the harshness of winter. *Cousinat* comprises chestnuts and helpings of cream, *ouillade* is of cabbage and beans, while *oulade* is *ouillade* with the addition of pork or sausage. Sausages and puddings are popular, too, the area's *charcuterie* being among the most distinctive in France. Pâtés and foie gras, based on goose, duck and chicken can also be found in abundance. The dishes are often flavoured with fungi from the high forests – chanterelle, morel and cep mushroom.

The upland areas also produce excellent cheeses. Roquefort, just outside the Languedoc border, needs no introduction, but there are a number of excellent local cheeses that are also worth trying. Bleu des Causses is a blue cheese made from cows' milk: it is less subtle and creamy than Roquefort, but certainly worthwhile. Local goats' milk cheeses should also be tried. Invariably these are made by a local farmer rather than a bulk producer, so watch out for the signs as you travel around. In restaurants, *flaunes* will sometimes be seen: these are pastry cases filled with one of the local cheeses.

Nearer the coast, fish dishes are popular. No surprise there, though it is surprising how little inland they travel, most being available only with sight of the Mediterranean. *Bouillabaisse*, the typical Provençal fish stew of white fish, herbs and garlic, is also found in Languedoc, together with a local fish speciality, *brandade de morue*, a thick stew of salted cod, milk and olive oil, heavily seasoned with herbs and garlic.

For dessert, the high hills of Languedoc offer *marrons glacés*, the typical chestnut luxury, while the plains offer *tartes*, fruit flans using the abundance of orchard and soft fruits. Try the local cherries and *myrtilles* (bilberries).

To wash this cuisine down there are the wines of Languedoc. Those who start their journey in the Ardèche and head south will be pampered by the wines of the Côtes du Rhône: Châteauneuf-du-Pape, one of France's great wines comes from the Rhône's eastern bank, just over the water from Gard. By comparison, the Languedocian wines are *vin ordinaire*, though the reputation of the AOC Côteaux du Languedoc is rising. Another notable is the *blanquette* of Limoux, a sparkling wine whose production pre-dates that of champagne. Or so it is said. In general, though, it is best to turn the lack of reputation of the local wines to advantage. As you drive around the area elaborate signs will frequently invite you to a local *cave* where local vintages can be tasted and bought inexpensively. That is the best way to find that hidden delight that has so far eluded the taste of the wine writers.

Hérault

The River Hérault rises on the flank of Mont Aigoual in the Cévennes National Park. It flows past the Grotte des Demoiselles, a fine cave carved out of the limestone of the Causses, then virtually defines the southern edge of the Causse du Larzac to reach St Guilhem-le-Désert, one of France's most celebrated villages. The river next heads across the fertile plain to the west of Montpellier before reaching the Mediterranean. In the course of its flow the river therefore defines the *département* it names, for Hérault is a *département* of contrasts, of wooded valleys, dry plateaux, fertile plains and holiday coastline; a *département* that offers something to suit the taste of all visitors.

MONTPELLIER

The best early view of Montpellier is seen by visitors exiting the A9 at 'Montpellier Est' and heading into the city on the D21. The road goes over the River Lez and reveals the stunning Esplanade de l'Europe, part of the new and splendid Antigone quarter which covers the 100 acres (40 hectares) of an old French army parade ground. Two squares provide a focus – the curiously named Place du Nombre d'Or (Golden Number Square) and the cypress-shaded Place du Millénaire (Millennium Square, a name more in keeping with the area's modernity).

The city to the west of the Antigone has a surprisingly short history for being so close to Roman Provence. It enters history in the tenth century as one a pair of local villages, then, around the year 1000, its reputation as a place for medicinal herbs led to the setting up of a medical school. The school grew in importance and influence throughout the Middle Ages, Rabelais studying there in the 1530s, and is still one of the greatest areas of French medical learning.

In 1204 the town passed to the Kingdom of Aragon and on the death of its king, to one of his sons as part of the short lived kingdom of Majorca. This move spared its inhabitants the excesses of the Albigensian Crusade, though the town did eventually become part of France, being sold to the French king in 1349. However the townsfolk were not inclined to bend the knee too readily to the Crown, becoming a site of Occitan culture and independence and, later, of Protestantism. Each can be seen as a rebellion against the Establishment and while the first was merely viewed as an irritant, the second was suppressed harshly during the Wars of Religion. In 1622 Louis XIII arrived in person to witness the final battle for control of Montpellier, during which much of the medieval town was destroyed.

The rebuilding, in fine Renaissance style, gave the city an excellent new look, and much of this remains in the old quarter. This old area is often claimed to be called the Ecusson from the old term for a crenellated wall (hence the term 'escutcheon'), but to most Montpellierians it is Le Clapas, the rubble, though the term is an affectionate,

tongue-in-cheek one as 'the rubble' has definite charms.

The old city lies between the Place de la Comédie and the Arc de Triomphe at the entrance to the Gardens of Peyrou. The Place, named for the Théatre - a fine late nineteenth-century building - at its western end, is called L'Ouef by locals, though the name was apparently more realistic a century ago than it is today. L'Ouef is now more rectangular than egg-shaped. In front of the theatre stands a fountain of the Three Graces, while at the eastern end there is a more modern work, with three bronze titans waist deep in a water trough. The Place is the hub of Montpellier life, a broad pedestrian square lined with cafés, the clientele enjoying both the sunshine and the entertainment from street performers.

From the Place's eastern end bear right for the short step to Antigone's shopping complex of Le Polygone, or bear left to the Esplanade Charles de Gaulle. The Esplanade heads north, a broad, tree-shaded promenade that continues the theme of L'Ouef. The left edge of the Esplanade is formed by the Boulevards of Serail and Bonne-Nouvelle. Close to where these meet, about half-way along the Esplanade, **Musée Fabre** stands to the left.

Close to Musée Fabre is a pair of museums housed in the **Hôtel des Varennes**, a mid-eighteenth century mansion. **The Musée du Vieux Montpellier** has a collection of old plans and drawings of the city from medieval to more modern times, while **Musée Fougau** has a collection of objects and furniture illustrating nineteenth century city life.

Hôtel des Trésoriers de France, standing in the road of the same

Musée Fabre

François-Xavier Fabre was born in Montpellier in 1766 and was studying as an artist in Florence when the Revolution broke out in France. He remained in Florence, becoming a friend of the Countess of Albany (widow of Bonnie Prince Charlie, the Young Pretender) and inheriting her art collection on her death in 1824. Fabre donated the collection to his home city where it is housed in a former Jesuit College.

The museum, which enthralled Van Gogh when he was at Arles, has works by Veronese, Rubens, Joshua Reynolds and David, as well as works by Fabre himself. One floor houses the collection of Alfred Bruyas, another benefactor, and has a number of works by Delacroix and Courbet. Interestingly, many of the works are of Bruyas himself, the patron's idea of supporting art being to pay good artists for portraits. The idea seems a little self-indulgent, but has resulted in fine work.

name, was once the Hôtel de Lunaret, home of Jacques Coeur, the humble merchant who rose to be treasurer of France. Coeur eventually fell foul of the aristocracy who resented his influence and he lost his position over a trumped-up charge. But before that, at the height of his powers, he lived here, increasing the wealth of Montpellier and Languedoc and the King's revenue at the same time. The rebuilt *hôtel* now houses a museum (entrance in Rue Jacques Coeur) to the archaeology and history of the area.

Beside the cathedral stands the University's Faculty of Medicine housed in an old Benedictine monastery. Inside is a **Musée d'Anatomie**, with a collection of mummies, instruments and more macabre exhibits, and the **Musée Atger**, a collection of drawings amassed by Xavier Atger. It includes works by Fragonard, Vernet, Rubens and Van Dyck amongst others. A further museum, the **Musée de l'Infanterie** traces the development of infantry weapons from medieval times to the present day.

North of Hôtel des Varennes, Rue du Cannau has some of Montpellier's finest seventeenth century houses. Others can be found in Rue de Girone, which heads west to the cathedral, a sixteenth-century, though much restored, building with several fine works of art.

Continued on page 24...

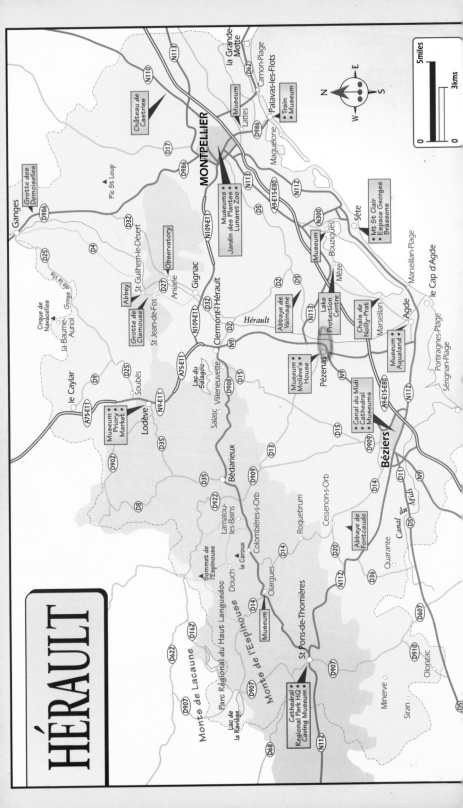

HÉRAULT

Ganges

Grotte des Demoiselles

D986

D25

Cirque de Navacelles

la Baume-Auriol

Gorge de la Vis

Pic St Loup

N113

N110

Château de Castries

D17

D986

D4

D32

St Guilhem-le-Désert

Abbey

D27

Aniane

Observatory

Gignac

MONTPELLIER

Museums
• Jardin des Plantes
• Lunaret Zoo

N109-E11

N113

Museum

Lattes

Train
• Museum

Palavas-les-Flots

Carnon-Plage

la Grande-Motte

D62

D986

Maguelone

N113

A9-E15-E80

N112

D5

N300

Sète

Mt St Clair
• Espace Georges Brassens

le Caylar

A75-E11

D9

D25

Soubès

Lodève

Museum
• Priory
• Market

D902

D35

N9-E11

A75-E11

St Jean-de-Fos

Grotte de Clamouse

D902

D35

Lac du Salagou

Salasc

Villeneuvette

D908

D15

Clermont-l'Hérault

Hérault

D2

N9

Abbaye de Valmagne

D2

D5

Museum

Bouzigues

Mèze

Lake Protection Centre

N113

Chais de Noilly-Prat

Marseillan

Marseillan-Plage

Agde

le Cap d'Agde

Portiragnes-Plage

Sérignan-Plage

N112

Museum
• Aqualand

Pézenas

Museum
• Molière's House

N9

Canal du Midi
• Cathedral
• Museums

Béziers

A9-E15-E80

N112

D11

N9

D909

D15

D13

Bédarieux

D909

D35

D8

D922

Lamalou-les-Bains

le Caroux

Douch

Colombières-s-Orb

Roquebrum

Cessenon-s-Orb

D14

Canal du Midi

Abbaye de Fontcaude

D20

Quarante

D36

D5

D14

Sommet de l'Espinouse

Monts de l'Espinouse

Olargues

D14

Museum

St Pons-de-Thomières

D907

Cathedral
• Regional Park HQ
• Caving Museum

N112

D68

Parc Régional du Haut Languedoc

Monts de Lacaune

D907

D622

D162

D907

Lac de la Raviège

Minerve

Siran

Olonzac

D910

D607

D5

N

W E

S

0   3kms
0   5miles

Above: *Montpellier in the early morning sunlight*
Below left: *Place de la Comédie, Montpellier*
Below right: *Arc de Triomphe, Montpellier*

Jardin des Plantes

Beside the Faculty of Medicine is the **Jardin des Plantes**, a superb garden founded in 1593, making it the oldest botanical garden in France. The tree and shrub collection covers both temperate and tropical plants and includes a good range of Languedocian species. The Orangery has a marble plaque inscribed Placandis Narcissae Manibus. This is not well understood, but seems likely to refer to Narcissa Young, daughter of the English poet Edward Young who loved the garden. She had been brought to Montpellier to assist recovery from TB, but died and may have been buried here. Because of this sad, but romantic, story the gardens became popular with lovers, the crevices of the Tree of Secrets at the highest point being used for the exchange of illicit love letters.

South of the cathedral is Place de la Canourgue where there are several fine mansions. From there it is a short step to the Promenade du Peyrou. The Promenade, with its formal gardens, is reached at the Arc de Triomphe. The arch, erected at the end of the seventeenth century, is a fine work, but has reliefs depicting Louis XIV's victories and his revocation of the Edict of Nantes in 1685. This monumental piece of crassness must have really endeared the king to the populace of Montpellier.

They were presumably equally enamoured of the huge equestrian statue of the king that stands in the middle of the Promenade. The statue is a replacement, the original having been broken up during the Revolution. That was the latest in a series of disasters. The story goes that when the sculptor realized he had forgotten to include the king's stirrups he killed himself and during the transport of the work from Paris to Montpellier it fell into a river.

From the Arc de Triomphe, Rue Foch and Rue de la Loge can be followed back to Place de le Comédie, though there are fine houses to be seen in the streets of the old quarter to the south (that is, to the right). South again is the Tour de la Babote the last of the twenty-five towers that once protected the medieval city walls.

Montpellier

Musée Fabre

39 Boulevard Bonne-Novelle
Open: All year, daily except Monday 9am-5.30pm (5pm Saturday and Sunday).
☎ 04 67 14 83 00.

Musée du Vieux Montpellier

Hôtel de Varennes, 2 Place Pétrarque
Open: All year, Tuesday to Saturday 9.30am-12noon, 1.30-5pm.
☎ 04 67 66 02 94.

Musée Fougau

Hôtel de Varennes, 2 Place Pétrarque
Open: All year, Wednesday and Thursday 3-6.30pm.
☎ 04 67 60 53 73.

Musée Languedocien

Hôtel des Trésoriers de France, 7 Rue Jacques Coeur
Open: All year, daily except Sunday 2-5pm (July and August 3-6pm).
☎ 04 67 52 93 03.

Musée d'Anatomie

Faculty of Medicine, 2 Rue des Écoles de Medecine
Open: All year, Monday to Friday 2.15-5pm.
☎ 04 67 60 73 71.

Musée Atger

Faculty of Medicine, 2 Rue des Écoles des Medicine
Open: All year except August, Monday, Wednesday and Friday 1.30-5pm.
☎ 04 67 66 27 77.

Musée de l'Infanterie

Caserne Guillault
Open: All year, daily except Monday 2-6pm.
☎ 04 67 07 21 39.

Jardin des Plantes (Botanical Garden)

Open: All year, daily except Monday 10am-7pm
(October to March 10am-5pm).
☎ 04 67 63 43 22.

AROUND MONTPELLIER

Montpellier is an excellent base for touring the southern tip of the Causses, the Camargue and the coast to the west of Aigues-Mortes, and, of course, the local area. Lunaret Zoo lies in the northern suburbs. It is really a wildlife park with free roaming zebra, bison etc together with a good collection of local animals. There is also an aviary of tropical birds.

Below: Palavas-les-Flots

To the south of Montpellier lies a series of *étangs*, brackish lagoons separated from the sea by sand bars. To explore them, take the D986 through **Lattes**, where a Roman necropolis has been discovered.

There is a small museum here (**Musée Archéologique Henri Prades**) which exhibits the finds from this site and other prehistoric and Gallo-Roman sites in the area. Beyond Lattes the road crosses the

*Above: **Vineyards and oyster farms, view to Sète***

Étang de Pérols to reach **Palavas-les-Flots**, a delightful, old-fashioned coastal resort.

Palavas - the addition to the name means 'the waves' - is popular with Montpellierians at weekends, although many of them continue to **Carnon-Plage** where the more modern pleasures of beach and café have totally taken over. Many years ago the folk of Montpellier travelled to Palavas on a miniature train, a train that became famous for the drawings the French humorist Albert Dubout made of it and its passengers. The original train has long gone, but a new one, just like the cartoons, has been built. There is also a museum to Dubout's work in a reconstructed eighteenth-century tower set up on an island in the

Étang du Levant. Visiting requires a boat ride, which Dubout would doubtless have found amusing.

Maguelone is thought to have been founded by the Greeks in the 2nd century AD and was certainly occupied by the Saracens in the eighth century. Later the town grew prosperous on the production of salt, a monastery was built and several Popes visited the site, entranced by its air of peace and holiness. The cathedral dates from the twelfth century when the town became the seat of the local bishop. Sadly the rise in importance of Montpellier meant that the bishop moved there.

Today only the cathedral remains, standing peacefully among a cluster of trees at the tip of a spit of land thrust into the Étang de l'Arnel. At

• CHÂTEAUX NEAR MONTPELLIER •

Close to Montpellier are a series of châteaux built as *folies* - summer retreats - by rich city folk. **Château d'O**, an eighteenth century mansion open only for events, is now used for concerts. It has beautiful grounds in which stand a collection of statues that once stood in the Château de la Mosson to the south. The latter was renowned for the luxury of its furnishings and decorations, but after its owners had been thrown out during the Revolution it was turned into a soap factory.

To the south-east of the city is **Château de Flaugergues,** which dates from 1696, and has a good collection of furnishings including seventeenth-century Flemish tapestries. Visits include a tasting of the estate's wine.

Château de Flaugergues: Open: Interior: July and August, daily except Monday 2.30-6.30pm.
Park: All year, daily except Sunday 9am-12.30pm, 2.30-7pm.
☎ 04 99 52 66 37.

Château de la Mogère is a newer building, dating from the early eighteenth century. It, too, is well furnished and also houses a good collection of paintings.

Château de la Mogère: Open: June to September daily 2.30-6.30pm; October-May Saturdays and Sundays 2.30-6.30pm.
☎ 04 67 65 72 01.

To the east, on the N110, is the **Château de Castries** that was not a *folie*. It was built in the sixteenth century, partially destroyed during the Revolution, but lovingly restored, and is worth a visit. It is still owned by the Castries family who originally built it (perhaps the most famous member of the family was the commander of the French army at Dien Bien Phu in Vietnam in 1954) and is excellently furnished. The gardens are superb and include a fountain supplied by a $4^1/_2$ mile (7km) aqueduct.

Château de Castries: Open: All year except mid-December to mid-January.
Interior: Guided tours at 2.45pm, 4pm and 5.15pm.
Park: daily 2.30-5.30pm.
☎ 04 67 70 68 86.

one time this spit continued as a causeway to the mainland, but was severed during the construction of the Canal du Rhône. Close by there are good rocky beaches, but this section of coast suffers, in summer, from the *Malaigue*, an all pervading smell of rotting vegetation as the plant life of the *étang* dies. The water is oxygen-starved, a situation that worsens as the temperature rises.

To the east of Carnon is **La Grande-Motte** a town that could hardly be more different from Maguelone. In the early 1960s the local planners decided to make a contemporary architectural statement on an area of land (*grande motte* = big lump) close to Aigues-Mortes. The architect, Jean Balladur, created a series of pyramids to house the shops and hotels of the new resort. The whole thing is great fun, though architectural purists may find it a little dated.

To the south, **Sète** is a charming place, the combination of canals and working port, together with fine views from **Mont St Clair**, good restaurants and cafés, and a complete lack of frills or pretensions making it one of the best coastal towns in the whole Languedoc. The town is mentioned as early as the ninth century, though its real history starts only with the building of the Canal du Midi in the late seventeenth century. Needing a terminal port it was decided to build one at this naturally defended spot, rather than at the other end of the Bassin de Thou where more building work would have been needed.

Ironically, within 40 years of Sète's construction the English had captured the port. That was in 1710, the occupying force's intention be-

ing to provide support to the Protestant Camisards. They were soon evicted. Thereafter, Sète became a peaceful, but industrous place, expanding to become France's biggest Mediterranean fishing port and one of its main commercial ports, with regular visits from freighters and tankers. This activity gives the place its busy, work-a-day air, one that enlivens any walk along the quays that line the sides of the small network of canals and basins. The best of the canals is **Canal de Sète** that bisects the town. The canal is the setting for one of the most vibrant of all Languedocian festivals, the **Joutes Nautiques**.

A more moving festival takes place on St Peter's Day. Then, a statue of the saint, the patron saint of fishermen, is carried from the church of St Louis to the canal and transported by barge to the fishing port. There it is transferred on to a flower-decked trawler. The boat is blessed and the flowers are thrown into the sea in memory of all sailors who have drowned. Many of the drowned are buried in the Cimitière Marin, the seamen's cemetery, at the base of **Mont St Clair**.

Beside the cemetery stands **Musée Paul Valéry**. Valéry, one of France's best loved poets, was born in Sète. The museum has a collection of memorabilia as well as collections on the history of the town and the water jousting.

Another son of the town was Georges Brassens, the folk singer, political activist and friend of Jean-Paul Sartre. He is remembered in a collection of memorabilia at the Espace (Centre) to him on Mont St Clair. There are marvellous views from Mont St Clair: follow Promenade de la Corniche, with fine sea

These water jousts - which also take place at Agde and Palavas - are held in August and attract large crowds. The two contestants, resplendent in white and holding 10ft (3m) lances and shields, stand on the *tintaines* (raised, elongated platforms) at the front of long rowing boats. The boats are rowed by ten oarsmen, also dressed in white. One boat is decorated in red and carries a red flag, the other is likewise arrayed in blue. To the accompaniment of musicians in each of the boats the crews sing an old jousting song and row at each other at high speed. The winner is the jouster who does not get wet. A large crowd watches and cheers and a great deal of fun is had by all.

views, and Avenue du Tennis to reach the **Parc Panoramique des Pierres Blanches**. From the viewpoint there is a great view of the Bassin de Thau, one of the largest lakes in Languedoc and home to huge oyster and mussel farms, the breeding frames making an interesting sight.

Places to Visit

South of Montpellier

Parc Zoologique de Lunaret

Rue de Val de Montferrand, Montpellier
Open: May to mid-September, daily 8am-7pm; mid-September to April, daily 8am-5.30pm.
☎ 04 67 63 27 23.

Musée Archéologique Henri Prades

Route de Pérols, Lattes
Open: All year daily except Tuesday 10am-12noon, 2-5.30pm.
☎ 04 67 99 77 20.

Espace Georges Brassens

67 Boulevard Camille Blanc, Sète
Open: All year daily 10am-12noon, 2-6pm (7pm June to September).
☎ 04 67 53 32 77.

Petit Train Albert Dubout

Palavas-les-Flots
Departures July and August, daily every 30 minutes 4pm-12midnight; April to June and September, daily except Monday 2-7pm (8pm in June).
☎ 04 67 68 56 41.

Musée Albert Dubout

Palavas-les-Flots
Embark from Quai Paul-Cinq
Open: July and August, daily 4pm-midnight; May, June and September, daily except Monday 2-7pm; April and October, daily except Monday 2-6pm; November to March, Saturday and Sunday 2-6pm.
☎ 04 67 68 58 41 or 04 67 07 73 82.

Musée Paul Valéry

Rue François Desnoyer, Sète
Open: July and August, daily 10am-12noon, 2-6pm; September to June, daily except Tuesday 10am-12noon, 2-6pm.
☎ 04 67 46 20 98.

SOUTH WEST OF MONTPELLIER

At Bouzigues there is a museum to the shellfish trade that explains the intricacies of conchyculture. Nearby, Mèze is one of the main places for shellfish production. It is possible to buy oysters and mussels direct from the farmers, but the visitor needs a strong stomach as the smell can be overpowering. The Station de Lagunage, an environmental protection pilot scheme, has an aquarium of local fish and details on projects to protect the *étang* and the sea from pollution.

Inland from Mèze the **Abbaye de Valmagne** stands in a circle of pines at the edge of the Hérault plain. It is one of the best preserved abbeys in Languedoc, a lovely, red stone building dating from the twelfth century. The abbey cloisters contain the real treasure, an octagonal pavilion enclosing a tall fountain. A romantic eighteenth-century poet named it the Fontaine d'Amour and it is easy to see why.

From Mèze the main road, the D51, draws away from the *étang*, but then reaches it again at **Marseillan**, a very old town that drew its first inhabitants and its name from Marseille some 2,500 years ago. Then it would have been a fishing or small commercial port. Today vineyards and the production of Noilly-Prat supply work for the villagers. Those interested in knowing more about the history and production of the dry vermouth aperitif can visit the **Chais de Noilly-Prat.**

Marseillan-Plage is one of the most popular of local beaches. It has beautiful sand and the sea is less polluted than almost anywhere else on the Mediterranean coast. How-ever, the beach does tend to be a little crowded, and the village behind, such as it is, is a characterless mix of camp sites and beach shops.

Agde, to the west of Marseillan, was also a Greek foundation in the sixth century BC, though they called it Agatha after one of their plethora of gods (Agatha Tyche). Even today the townsfolk of Agde are called Agathois. That name is also given to the town museum which explores its history and the folklore and traditions of the Agathois. One of the collections is of fishermen's equipment, Agde having been a port before the sea slipped south-wards marooning it inland.

Le Cap d'Agde, like La Grande Motte, dates from the 1960s though here the design is based on more traditional houses. The visitor can climb the volcanic **Mont St Loup,** which provided the stone for Agde, enjoy the beaches - which really are exceptional - explore the port, almost completely enclosed with innumerable interesting nooks and crannies, or visit such diverse places as the **Musée de l'Éphèbe** and **Aqualand.**

The museum takes its name from the bronze statue of a boy discovered in 1964 at the bottom of the Hérault and known as the Éphèbe d'Agde. The other exhibits of the museums have also been collected by the new techniques of underwater archaeology. In complete contrast, Aqualand is a large site dedicated to water based amusements, with several swimming pools and a bewildering array of water slides. There are also cafés and bars.

Continued on page 36...

The Destruction of Béziers

In 1209 Béziers was shattered by one of the most appalling incidents in French history. The Albigensian Crusade had just begun, the crusading army under Arnold Amaury, Bishop of Citeaux, arriving at its first city in Cathar country. Records show that there were 200 Cathars in Béziers, but when ordered to do so, the Catholic townsfolk declined to hand them over to the Crusaders. The Bishop therefore gave the order to destroy the city. When asked how the soldiers should distinguish the heretics from the true believers he gave his infamous reply – 'Kill them all. The Lord will know his own'. The soldiers began slaughtering the townsfolk who fled in terror to seek sanctuary in the cathedral and other churches. These were fired, incinerating the occupants. By the end of the day Béziers had been virtually wiped off the map. Making his report to Pope Innocent III, the Bishop seemed almost dismayed that his soldiers had been able to kill only 20,000 people.

Cathedral & Pont Vieux

Enjoying the beach & sea, Marseillan-Plage

Canal du Midi

Pézenas, inland from Agde, was a Roman town, a place of wool spinning and cloth-making, but it achieved its greatest fame in the fifteenth to seventeenth centuries when it was the seat of the Estates-General of Languedoc making it the effective capital of south-west France. This position brought the aristocrats and wealthy merchants to the town and here they built their grand houses.

After the Revolution the town went into a steep decline, but for the visitor this was its salvation, the old town being virtually a museum to architectural styles from the Renaissance to 1700, with over seventy listed buildings. During the years 1653-1656 the great French comedy playwright Molière stayed in Pézenas and for a time the **Hôtel d'Alfonce** was his theatre. The house is open to visitors. Those interested in finding out more about the history of the town and of Molière's stay here should visit the **Musée Vulliod-St-Germain** housed in a fine sixteenth-century house.

From Pézenas the N9 speeds the visitor to **Béziers**. The defensive mound above the River Orb on which the city sits was occupied before the Romans arrived in southern France and grew in importance until 1209.

After 1209 Béziers is little heard of for 400 years. Only with the building of **the Canal du Midi** did its fortunes revive. The builder of the canal, Pierre-Paul Riquet, was born in Béziers, the grateful citizens having raised a statue to him in the middle of the delightful Allées Paul-Riquet, a wide promenade shaded by plane trees. At its south-

The Canal du Midi

Pierre-Paul Riquet was not only the engineer of the canal but the financier as well, obtaining the money from the profits he made as Languedoc's *fermier général*. This job - literally a tax farmer - involved buying the right to collect an area's taxes, and then keeping anything collected over that figure. Riquet must have been good at this form of farming as the Canal took 12,000 men 15 years to complete, its 150 miles (240km) of waterway involving the building of over 100 locks and innumerable bridges. Sadly Riquet died just before the waterway was opened.

By a meandering route the canal links Sète (and the Mediterranean) with Toulouse and the River Garonne which is navigable all the way to the Atlantic. Though it is little used today by commercial traffic, it is still open all along its length. With its tree shade, wildlife and peaceful look at areas of Languedoc that the main tourist highways do not reach, the canal is an excellent way of exploring the region. Boats can be hired at virtually all the towns along the way.

ern end the promenade runs into the romantically named **Plateau des Poètes**, a lovely public park where the shade is offered by more exotic trees including Californian sequoias and Lebanon cedars.

Going the other way along Allées Paul-Riquet - follow Avenue Foch, then turn left - the visitor reaches the church of St Aphrodise. This was the site of the Bézier's first cathedral, named - or so it is said - for an early Christian who rode into the Roman town on a camel (a camel is now the city's symbol) and tried to convert the inhabitants. The Romans cut off his head and threw it down a well - which seems an extraordinarily unhygienic thing to do - but the well water rose, bringing the head back to the surface where the decapitated body scooped it up and carried it to this spot. There, head and body disappeared.

When viewed from the old bridge over the Orb, Béziers seems to be topped by an angular castle. It comes as a surprise to many visitors that this is the city's cathedral. The present building was started in 1215, just six years after its destruction, a fact that makes one marvel at the strength of the faith of thirteenth-century Languedocians. Outside it is overwhelmingly fortress-like, seemingly constructed to remind and intimidate the townsfolk. Inside it is much more forgiving. The beautiful vaulted cloister incorporates what remains of the earlier building.

Close to the cathedral is the **Musée des Beaux-Arts**. The museum occupies two fine old houses, Hôtel Fabrégat and Hôtel Fayet. Hôtel Fabrégat has a good collection of paintings with work by such no-tables as Utrillo and Dufy, while Hôtel Fayet has a collection of nineteenth-century paintings. To the south there is a third museum. **Musée du Biterrois** is housed in an early eighteenth-century barracks and has collections on local archaeology, folklore and traditions and the natural history of the area.

North-west of Béziers is **Fontcaude Abbey**. The abbey was founded in 1154, taking its name from a nearby hot spring (*fontaine chaude*). It was finally abandoned during the Revolution. Today the remains of the church and cloisters offer a peaceful interlude after the noise and energy of the coast. A museum on the site illustrates the history of the site.

To the south of Béziers is a section of coastline that is still relatively unknown to visitors. Here old fishing ports and beautiful beaches can be found that are still free of the commercialism that has affected some resorts to the east. **Portiragnes-Plages, Sérignan-Plage** and **Valras-Plage** (the latter the largest and busiest of them all) are all worth visiting for a quieter afternoon.

Musée de l'Etang de Thau (Shellfish Museum)

Bouzigues
Open: June to August, daily 10am-12noon, 2-7pm; September to May, daily 10am-12noon, 2-5pm (6pm March to May and September).
☎ 04 67 78 33 57 or 04 67 78 35 85.

Station de Lagunage (Lake Protection Centre)

Mèze
Open: July and August, daily 10am-7pm; September to June, daily 2-6pm.
☎ 04 67 46 64 94.

Valmagne Abbey

Nr Mèze
Open: mid-June to mid-September, daily 10am-12noon, 2.30-6.30pm; mid-September to mid-June, daily 2-6pm.
☎ 04 67 78 06 09.

Chais de Noilly-Prat

Marseillan
Open: guided tours, daily 10am-12noon, 2.30-7pm (6pm October to April).
☎ 04 67 77 20 15.

Musée Agathois

Rue de la Fraternité
Agde
Open: All year, daily except Tuesday 10am-12noon, 2-6pm.
☎ 04 67 94 82 51.

Aqualand, Le Cap d'Agde

Musée de l'Éphèbe

Le Cap d'Agde
Open: July and August, daily 9.30am-12.30pm, 2.30-6.30pm; September to June, daily except Tuesday and Sunday morning 9am-12noon, 2-6 pm.
☎ 04 67 94 69 60.

Aqualand

Le Cap d'Agde
Open: early-June to mid-September, daily 10am-7pm.
☎ 04 67 26 85 94.

Hôtel d'Alfonce

32 Rue Conti
Pézenas
Open: mid-June to mid-September, 10am-12noon, 2-6pm.
☎ 04 67 98 10 38.

Musée de Vulliod-St-Germain

3 Rue Albert Paul Allies
Pézenas
Open: July and August, daily 10am-12noon, 3-7pm, September to June, daily except Monday and Sunday morning 10am-12noon, 2-5pm.
☎ 04 67 98 90 59.

Musée des Beaux-Arts

Béziers
Hôtel Fabrégat
Place de la Revolution
Open: daily except Monday and Sunday morning 9am-12noon, 2-6pm.

Hôtel Fayet

9 Rue du Capus
Open: Easter to Christmas, Tuesday-Friday 9am-12noon, 2-6pm.
☎ 04 67 28 38 78.

Musée du Biterrois

Béziers
Open: June to September, daily except Monday 10am-7pm;
October to May, daily except Monday 9am-12noon, 2-6pm.
☎ 04 67 36 71 01.

Abbaye de Fontcaude

Nr Cazedarnes
Open: June to September, daily except Sunday morning 10am-12noon, 2.30-7pm; October to December and February to May, Monday, Saturday and Sunday 2.30-4.30pm.
☎ 04 67 38 23 85.

NORTH OF MONTPELLIER

From the city the D986 heads towards the Causse Larzac and Mont Aigoual. This is a delightful road, crossing the Hérault Plain before reaching the more scenically impressive country at the southern edge of the Cévennes National Park. Just before reaching St Martin-de-Londres turnings to the left and right give access to interesting, but very different sites. To the right is Pic St Loup, which despite its low summit (at 2,158ft - 658m) is a fabulous viewpoint because of the even lower plain from which it rises.

Continuing along the D986 the visitor soon reaches the **Grotte des Demoiselles**. The cave's name derives from the fairies the local folk thought lived in it, such openings into the mountains invariably being seen as entrances to the underworld by superstitious medieval folk. The sheer size of the cave is awesome - the main cavern is 400ft (120m) long and 165ft (50m) high - and though some of the formations have fanciful names (in the 'Cathedral' there is one called the 'Virgin and Child') there is no doubting their beauty.

Beyond the cave is **Ganges**, a town once famed for the manufacture of silk stockings. Stocking-making is till carried on here, but now they are chiefly of nylon. From the town the main road (the D999) goes north to Le Vigan and Mont Aigoual and east towards Nîmes. To stay in Hérault, take the D25, a road that drifts into and out of Gard as it follows the **Gorge de Vis** - an aptly named river, as *vis* means corkscrew. The most striking feature is the Cirque de Navacelles (see Chapter on Gard). The best viewpoint for the *cirque* is **Le Baume-Aurial** (in Hérault) on the D130.

Lavognes and the Transhumance

The limestone of the *causses*, being permeable, has few streams and pools for animals to drink. To allow their flocks and herds to drink the *causse* farmers therefore created *lavognes*, mud-lined depressions that were filled naturally by rain or by way of piped systems. The transhumance occurs around All Saints Day when the flocks and herds are driven down from the *causses* to lower, more sheltered, pastures. Nowadays the journey is usually by lorry, but occasionally - and most frequently on Larzac - the animals, dressed for the occasion with flags, flowers and pom-poms, are herded in old style.

The D25 crosses the **Causse de Larzac**, the largest of the *causses* and the one on which the visitor is most likely to see a *lavogne* or the transhumance.

The D25 reaches the N9 at **Soubès**. To the right from here is **Le Caylar** with a fine collection of medieval houses, a clock tower that is all that remains of the old town walls and the **Chapelle du Rocastel**, a pretty little Romanesque building. On the outskirts of the town are a series of rocks, weirdly carved by millennia of wind and rain. These give the village its name, *caylar* meaning rocky in the Oc language.

Turning left at Soubès takes the visitor to **Lodève**, a busy little town with an exciting Saturday market. The town's prosperity was based on cloth made from the wool of Larzac sheep, an industry that lasted several hundred years and ceased relatively recently. Within the town the Pont de Montfort is a fine Gothic bridge over the River Soulondres. Also worthy of note is the cathedral, a thirteenth-century building that was modified to act as a fortress during the Hundred Years War. **Hôtel de Fleury**, built in the seventeenth century as a palace for Cardinal de Fleury, houses the town museum with exhibits on the geology and the pre-history of the area. It also has a superb collection of fossil footprints.

Close to Lodève is the **Priory of St Michel de Grandmont**. The Priory dates from the late twelfth century and is the only surviving building in France of the Grandmont movement. It has been restored to something approaching its original magnificence and occupies a superb position with excellent views.

The Pont du Diable

On the D27 from Aniane is the **Pont du Diable**. It was built by the monks of St Guilhem in the eleventh century, though why it has acquired its distinctly non-monastic name is not clear. Probably, in time its origins were forgotten and locals began to believe in a supernatural builder. On the southern side of the bridge - which spans the River Hérault - a wide sweep of river has created a beach which, in summer, is well populated with bathers. The rocks below the bridge itself attract intrepid divers, while the Hérault Gorge, upstream, is the realm of canoeists and rafters. Visitors wanting to join in the fun should go to St Guilhem where various companies hire out equipment or offer trips.

Heading west from Montpellier along the N109, the journey is uneventful as far as **Gignac**. The town is famous for its Fête d'Ane (Festival of the Donkey) held on Ascension Day. The festival reminds the townsfolk of the donkey whose braying saved their ancestors from a surprise Saracen attack a thousand years ago. As part of the festivities some of the townsfolk dress as Saracens and are ceremonially defeated.

Nearby **Aniane** (follow the D32) is equally famous for the Branle de Chemise when the townsfolk walk in procession in nightgowns carrying candles. The reason for the festival is lost in the mists of time, no great surprise as Aniane is one of the oldest villages in the area, built at the edge of the Causse de Larzac where water which has run beneath the limestone springs back to the surface. Spring water still provides the village's supply. The **Aniane Observatory** is open to visitors who can see all the equipment and techniques that modern astronomy employs.

The road from the Pont du Diable to St Guilhem passes the **Grotte de Clamouse** another fine show cave. Clamouse is famed for its pure white formations and the delicacy of its stalactites. **St Guilhem-le-Désert** is one of the most picturesque villages in France and though its fame has resulted in it becoming a little too discovered and pretty, it is still a fine place. The 'desert' of the name is another reference to the secret valleys of the *causses*.

The abbey that now stands at the top of the village dates from the eleventh century. It is a fine building with remnants of its original frescoes still visible, but it is sad that

St Guilhem

Guilhem was a grandson of Charles Martel, a friend and general of Charlemagne. As a soldier he took Aquitane and repulsed the Saracens, but when his wife died he decided to retire to live as a hermit. History records the last meeting of the two men, each of them in tears, as they knew they would never see each other again. Charlemagne gave Guilhem a piece of the True Cross and he brought it here, founding a monastery and diverting a stream to keep it supplied with fresh water. Guilhem died in 812 and was buried in the church he raised.

those now responsible for its upkeep allowed the majority of the cloister to be dismantled and re-assembled in New York's Cloisters Museum. The village museum, housed in what was once the monastery's refectory, has many treasures from the abbey, including what is known as St Guilhem's sarcophagus, but which almost certainly pre-dates him by several centuries.

The village stands on one side of a ravine, its single street too narrow for vehicles. To make the most of a visit, walk up the road that takes vehicles to the car park at the top (if you have parked at the bottom). This road offers fine views of the village and leads to the abbey and museum, and the Place de la Liberté. From here, the road to the left is Rue de Bout du Monde, the Road to the End of the World. It is probably better to take the alley to Rue Chapelle des Penitents, turning right to walk through the village back to the Hérault gorge.

Pont du Diable

Insert: Gorge de E'Hérault,
near St Guilhem-le-Désert

North of Montpellier

Grotte des Demoiselles

Open: July and August, daily 10am-6pm; April to June and September, daily 9am-12noon, 2-7pm; October to March, daily 9.30-12noon, 2-5pm.
☎ 04 67 73 70 02.

Musée Cardinal-de-Fleury

Lodève
Open: daily except Monday, 9.30am-12noon, 2-6pm.
☎ 04 67 88 86 10.

Priory of St Michel de Grandmont

Nr Lodève
Open: Guided tours only, Easter to September, daily 10.30am-5pm; October to Easter, Sundays and public holidays at 3pm only.
☎ 04 67 44 09 31.

Géospace Observatoire d'Aniane

Open: Guided tours only. July and August, daily except Monday 10am-12noon, 2-6pm, September to June, Sunday 2-5pm.
☎ 04 67 03 49 49.

Grotte de Clamouse

Nr St Guilhem-de-Désert
Open: July and August, daily 10am-7pm; September, October and March to June, 10am-5pm, November to February, daily 12noon-5pm.
☎ 04 67 57 71 05.

Abbey Museum

St Guilhem-le-Désert
Open: July and August, daily 11am-12noon, 2.30-6.30pm; June and September, daily 2-6pm (5pm October to May).
☎ 04 67 57 71 45.

FURTHER WEST

From St Guilhem the Hérault can be followed all the way to Ganges, but the best it has to offer has already been seen, so return to Pont du Diable and bear right to St Jean de Fos and Montpeyroux. From here little lanes can be followed to Clermont l'Hérault, a quiet little town with a pleasant old quarter and a good thirteenth-century church. Close by is Lac du Salagou, a man-made lake that is popular with bathers, water-sports enthusiasts and anglers. The best of its beaches is on the eastern tip. A drive around the lake is worthwhile for the view across it, the blue water backed by the red hills of Roussillon is exceptional.

The lakeside drive reaches **Salasc,** a very pretty village with an exquisite fountain in the square. Outside the village there is a small collection of *roches ruiniformes*, though to see a better display it is necessary to go to **Mourèze**. The Cirque de Mourèze, while not as impressive as that at Navacelles, is nonetheless interesting and the rock piles that surround the village give it an unreal air. Close to the village, in Courtinals Park, a pre-Roman Gothic village has been reconstructed on a site known to have been used at that time. Close by is **Villeneuvette** a village built in 1670 for the manufacture of linen cloth. The old factory and houses are distinctly gloomy, the sign 'Honneur au Travail' ominous, but of late the village has been 're-discovered' and is becoming a focus for local artists and craftworkers.

From these three villages the D908 heads westwards to **Bédarieux** offering, from its high point before the drop down into the town, a stunning view of the hills of **Espinouse**. Bédarieux is a pleasant market town whose main square is named after a nineteenth-century painter, Pierre-Auguste Cot, who was born here.

Westwards is **Lamalou-les-Bains,** a good start for exploring the western end of the Monts de l'Espinouse. As the name implies, Lamalou is a small spa town, one which numbers Alphonse Daudet and André Gide, several counts and dukes and a Sultan of Morocco among former clients. Today it specializes in muscular problems and nervous disorders. The railway helped Lamalou's prosperity rise, but then helped it to fall as the trains took former visitors elsewhere. It is worth strolling out of the west end of the village to see the elegant church of St Pierre-de-Rhèdes, a twelfth-century Romanesque building that is claimed to be the most beautiful example of the style in central France.

From Lamalou the D908 leads westwards to **Colombières-sur-Orb**. From the bridge here a marked walk (*Sentier des Gorges*) leads to a fine gorge of the Orb river. It is only a short walk, allow about 40 minutes for the round trip, but well worth the effort. The Orb is a beautiful river for most of its length and the valley downstream of Colombières - followed by the D14, reached by going west along the D908 and turning left - follows its looping curves through another fine gorge. The road leads to **Roquebrun**, set on the river, and **Cessenon**.

The Devil and the Bellringer

Cessenon is said to derive its name from the time the Devil took a morning constitutional along the Orb valley. He was bothered by the noise of the village's church bell and finally shouted out 'Cesse'. To this the bellringer, recognizing the shouter, replied, equally loudly 'Non'.

Further along the D908 is **Olargues**, a village that can be reached by a longer, more difficult, but far more exciting and scenically splendid route. To follow this route, go north from Lamalou along the D180, following it over the Col de Madale and the Col des Avels.

Just after the latter, turn left to reach **Douch** a village that is little more than a huddle of stone cottages roofed by *lauzes*, split stones. The narrow alleys offer unexpected, and delightful, views of **Mont Caroux** and lead to a tiny Romanesque church. From Douch the peak of Mont Caroux (at 3,411ft - 1,040m) can be reached along a well-marked track (allow 2 hours for the round trip).

Our tour continues over the Col de l'Ourtigas into the very heart of the beautiful Monts de l'Espinouse. The highest point of the range, the aptly named **Sommet de l'Espinouse** (3,687ft – 1,124m) can be reached from Rec d'Agout, a farmhouse further along the road. The visitor is now at the heart of the **Haut Languedoc Regional Park**, created in 1972 to protect the flora and fauna of the forests and hills of this area of northern Languedoc. Much of the Park lies outside Languedoc, in the *département* of Tarn, part of the region of Midi-Pyrénées, but within the section of the park that lies in Hérault there are mouflon, wild boar and genet, short-toed eagle and, occasionally, Egyptian vultures. Continue through Agoudet and Cambon before crossing the Col de Fontfroide and the Col du Poirier, both excellent viewpoints. Beyond, on the D908, is Olargues.

Olargues is a beautiful village with a maze of cobbled alleyways, some running under the houses, a delightful eleventh-century bell-tower and an equally delightful twelfth-century humpback bridge. The village museum explores the local history, folklore and natural history.

Continue along the D908, still enjoying fine views to the Monts de l'Espinouse, to reach **St Pons-de-Thomières**, the 'capital' of Espinouse. The cathedral here is a fine building, started in the twelfth century, but with additions almost continuously since. St Pons is the seat of the Regional Park Authority, the offices being worth visiting if more information on the Park and its plant and animal life is required.

Also worthwhile is the **Musée de Préhistoric Régionale**. Neolithic and Bronze Age peoples seem to have settled in the local area in great numbers - such numbers that some experts believe the area represents a specific civilization. The museum has an excellent collection of finds, including a number of statue menhirs, carved standing stones, that were a feature of the 'civilization'.

Close to St Pons is another fine show cave. The **Grotte de la Devèze** was first explored by Louis Armand who gave his name to Lozère's Aven Armand. The cave is sometimes known as the Palace of the Glass Spinner so delicate and intricate are its formations. Close to the cave is the **Musée François de la Spéléologie** (the French Museum of Speleology) with items on the history of French caving and developments in techniques which will be of interest to both enthusiasts and those who never wish to go inside such places.

From St Pons the D907 (to Lacaune) can be used to explore the western edge of the Monts de l'Espinouse. The road crosses the hill range, then drops to **Lac de la Raviège**, a reservoir watersports site, before rising again to explore the Monts de Lacaune (also part of the Haut Languedoc Regional Park, but in Midi-Pyrénées). To the east of the lake, at **Fraisse-sur-Agout**

Fountain at Salasc

Haut Monervois is named from the pretty village of **Minerve**, an important site for centuries. Man has lived here since Paleolithic times and the first church was built in the fifth century (the present Romanesque church dates from the eleventh century). However, it was the fortifications and castle that made Minerve renowned in the early thirteenth century and it was there that the few survivors of the Béziers massacre of 1209 and other Cathars fled, pursued by the army of Simon de Montfort. De Montfort besieged the castle for two months, eventually forcing the Cathars to surrender by cutting off their water supply. Montfort prepared a fire for the heretics and was surprised that many threw themselves on to it. After the butchery of Béziers they may have decided it was the less painful option.

Little now remains of the fortifications, just an octagonal tower of the castle which the locals - with no apparent irony - call the *candela*. The town's Cathar past is reproduced in a series of dioramas in **Musée Hurepel**, in the appropriately named Rue des Martyrs, one of the most picturesque of Minerve's array of narrow alleys.

Musée Hurepel

Open: July and August, daily 11am-7pm; September and April to June, daily 2-6pm.
☎ 04 68 46 10 28.

The town's prehistory is explored in a separate museum, also in Rue des Martyrs, which also includes exhibits on local geology.

Village Museum

Open: July to mid-September, daily 10.30am-5.30pm; April to June, Monday-Saturday 2-5pm; Mid-September to March, Sunday 2-5pm.
☎ 04 67 89 47 98.

For real examples of how interesting that geology can be, take the D147 out of the village a short way to see two Ponts Naturels. This pair of tunnels was bored through the limestone on which the village sits by earlier *causses* of the River Cesse. The longer of the two tunnels is 820ft (250m) long and 98ft (30m) high at its highest point. Please note that the tunnels should only be explored in the very driest of weather.

there is an ecomuseum, the farm of Prat d'Alaric being stocked with tools and machinery which shows that for generations the way of working the land of the Espinouse has changed very little. South of St Pons lies the **Haut Minervois**, a final upland section of the Montagne Noire.

From Minerve it is worth exploring the Minervois, following minor roads to go deep into little visited country. One worthwhile destination is the **Chapelle des Centeilles** - to the north of **Siran,** a village southwest of Minerve - and **Olonzac**. The chapel is a remarkable survival, its fourteenth- and fifteenth-century frescoes being virtually intact.

Finally, at the extreme eastern edge of Minervois is **Quarante** where the church, a fine tenth century building, houses a treasury that includes a third-century marble sarcophagus and some superb fifteenth-century silverwork.

P l a c e s t o V i s i t

Western Hérault

Parc des Courtinals (Gallic Village)

Mourèze
Open: March to December, Saturday and Sunday 10am-6pm (open daily April to September).
☎ 04 67 96 08 42.

Village Museum

Olargues
Open: July to mid-September 10am-12noon, 4-7pm.
☎ 04 67 97 70 79 or 04 67 97 88 00.

Haut Languedoc Regional Park Office

13 Rue du Cloître
St Pons-de-Thomières
Open: Monday to Friday 10-11.30am, 3-5pm.
☎ 04 67 97 02 10.

Musée de Préhistoire Régionale

6 Rue du Barry
St Pons-de-Thomières
Open: mid-June to mid-September, daily 10am-12noon, 3-6pm; mid-September to mid-June, Wednesday, Saturday and Sunday 10am-12noon, 2.30-5.30pm Tuesday, Thursday and Friday 10am-12noon.
☎ 04 67 97 22 61.

Grotte de la Devèze/ Musée François de la Spéléologie

Nr St Pons-de-Thomières
Cave Open: July and August, daily 10am-6pm; September, October and March to June, daily 2-5pm.
Museum Open: July and August, daily 10am-6pm; Easter to June and September, daily 2-5pm; October, November and February to Easter Saturday and Sunday, 2-5pm.
☎ 04 67 97 03 24.

Ecomusée Prat d'Alaric

Fraisse-sur-Agout
Open: July to mid-September daily 3-6pm.
☎ 04 67 97 38 22.

2 Gard

Like Herault, Gard is named for a river, one that rises in the Cévennes and flows into the Rhône. On its journey it flows under the Pont du Gard, one of the most famous Roman remains in Europe and one often used as the symbol of Roman Provincia. For many visitors Pont du Gard, Roman Nîmes and the medieval town of Aigues-Mortes are part of Provence yet they actually lie within Languedoc, adding another dimension to this other south of France.

CÉVENNES NATIONAL PARK

The area of the Park within Gard includes Mont Aigoual, in the north-west of the *département* is a granitic mass, the last great peak of the Massif Central before the Mediterranean is reached. Over the peak, northward moving air from the Mediterranean, hot, dry air, meets colder, damper air moving south-eastward from the Atlantic. As a result rain falls on the peak on 166 days each year (on average) – every other day – a total of 90 inches (2.3m) annually. This high rainfall has named the peak, Aigoual from *aigualis*, local dialect for water.

Within the forests on its flanks red and roe deer, wild boar and mouflon (similar to domestic sheep, but thinner – the males having superb curved horns) roam. The deer and the mouflon were re-introduced to the area after extensive re-affor-estation, the Aigoual massif having become denuded of forest by the end of the last century, the trees making way for sheep. At that time the naturalist Georges Fabre recognised the importance of the forests both to the ecology and hydrology of the area and persuaded the French government to re-afforest the area.

There is a car park near the meteorological station on the 5,140ft (1,567m) summit of Mont Aigoual. The station – which houses an exhibition on French weather – helps record such data as 60 days annually of snow, 140 days of frost, winter winds of 65mph. And, of course, 166 days of rain. From the summit the view is excellent. On a clear day Mont Blanc and Mont Ventoux can be seen to the east, the Pyrenees to the west. Northward Mont Cantal is visible, while to the south is the Mediterranean. More locally there is a fine view of the Causses and the high Cévennes.

God's Garden

The top of Mont Aigoual is a mecca for walkers (there are several GRs) and also for mountain bikers, many of whom hire vehicles from local shops, are driven to the top and then cycle back down. These two groups get the best view of the flowers for which the massif is famous, but even car-borne visitors can follow one route, the Sentier des Botanists, a 20 minute walk which overlooks the **Hort-de-Dieu** (God's Garden), a small arboretum set up by Georges Fabre's botanist co-worker, Charles Flahault.

From the summit, go down to the **Col de la Séreyrède**, a surprisingly good viewpoint. The Col is crossed by the Draille d'Aubrac, a transhumance track that has been used for centuries. A 15-minute walk from

the col reaches the **Cascade de l'Hérault** where the waters of the Hérault drop in a pretty waterfall.

Going westwards from the col – take the D986 to Meyrueis – another fine show cave is reached. The **Abîme de Bramabiau** has been carved in the limestone of the Causse de Camprieu, one of the smaller plateaux that lie close to the four Grands Causses. It is unusual in being an *abîme*, an abyss or chasm, rather than a *grotte* or *aven*. The reason for this is the stream that exits from the cave mouth. The noise of this stream, which drops over a short waterfall, sounded, to the locals, like a bellowing ox, especially after the stream had been swollen by heavy rain: the cave's name means the Abyss of the Bellowing Ox.

The stream that created the cave, the Bonheur, sinks into the Causse de Camprieu some distance from the waterfall, heading down a 'conventional' *aven*. After chiseling out a series of passages and caverns the stream exits the cave, re-appearing above ground again. Such re-appearances are known as resurgences. It is highly unusual for show caves to be entered at the resurgence rather than the sink point and if there has been high rainfall the stream rises and access becomes impossible. The caves are pretty, the underground stream adding to the beauty. The cave entrance is reached by a walk from the ticket office.

Just before the Abîme is reached, a small road goes off left to the **Gorges du Trévezel**. This delightful gorge is truly wild and, in parts, remarkably narrow. At the Pas de l'Ase (Pass of the Donkey in the local dialect) the gorge narrows to just 115ft (35m).

South from the Col de la Séreyrède is **L'Esperou**, a village with an enviable position, protected from north winds by Mont Aigoual, but facing south, towards the Mediterranean. From the village the D986 goes east to **Valleraugue**, while the D48 heads south to Le Vigan. Valleraugue is a market town at the heart of an apple growing area. From it a famous walk – one that takes a long day if return is by the same route – follows the **Sentier des 4,000 Marches**, the Walk of 4,000 Steps (a somewhat optimistic title) to the summit of Mont Aigoual.

Le Vigan is famous in France for having been the birthplace of two heroic soldiers, Louis d'Assas and Sergeant Triaire whose statues adorn the town. Of more general interest is the **Musée Cévenol** set close to the river at the Vieux Pont, a very picturesque thirteenth-century bridge. Cévenol is the name given to inhabitants or villages within, or close to, the Cévennes National Park. The museum, housed in an old silk mill, has a good collection of items that illustrate the history of village life within the Cévennes. It includes a collection of locally made silk clothes dating from the nineteenth century.

South-west of Le Vigan is the Causse du Larzac, the largest of the Grands Causses, covering around 400 square miles (1,000 square kilometres). Most of the Causse lies in Hérault, but one of its most beautiful, and distinctive, features lies in Gard: the **Cirque de Navacelles**. The cirque is best viewed from one of two viewpoints: La **Baume-Auriol** lies to the south, the **Belvédère Nord** (as might be expected) to the north. Interestingly, the Vis has created another cirque, the Cirque de Vissec, just a short distance to the north-west.

Cirques

Occasionally, a *causse* river, one that has already cut a gorge, will create a meander, or loop. Now, if the river cuts through a section of limestone to create a shorter, straighter flow path the old loop will be left. In non-permeable rock areas, such 'dead' loops remain filled with water to form ox-bow lakes. In the *causses*, where water does not lie on the surface, the old meander is soon left as a dry loop or *cirque*. The best examples of *cirques* are here at Navacelles and at Mourèze in Hérault.

East of Mont Aigoual is the southeastern section of the Cévennes National Park, a glorious area for the walker and for the visitor who wishes to explore little-used roads. The best starting points for exploration are **St Hippolyte-du-Fort**, to the south, and St Jean-du-Gard to the north.

St Hippolyte-du-Fort is a charming town, set where the high Cévennes peaks reach the Languedoc plain. It has an array of fine seventeenth- and eighteenth-century houses and two old towers, all that now remain of the medieval town wall. From the eighteenth century this area of Languedoc was known for silk making: it is said that local women wore pouches around their necks so that the eggs of the

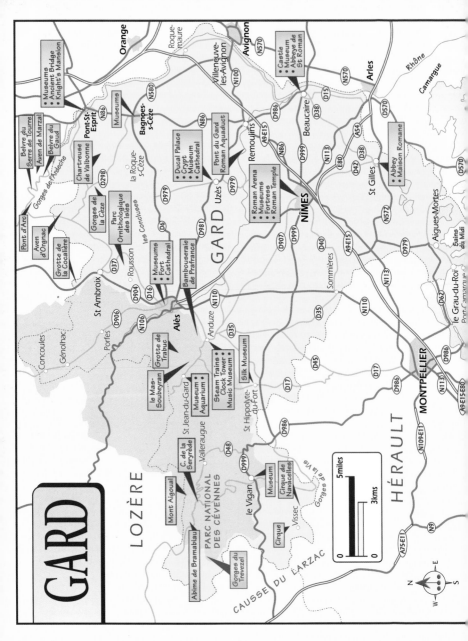

The map shows the GARD region with the following labeled locations:

- Museums • Ancient Bridge • Knight's Mansion
- Belvre du Serre de Tourre
- Aven de Marzal
- Belvre du Gaud
- Museums
- Chartreuse de Valbonne (D298)
- Pont-St-Esprit
- Bagnols-s-Cèze
- la Roque-s-Cèze
- Pont d'Arc
- Aven d'Orgnac
- Grotte de la Cocalière
- Gorges de l'Ardèche
- Gorges de la Cèze
- Parc Ornithologique des Isles
- les Conoluses
- St Ambroix
- Rousson
- Museums • Fort • Cathedral
- Bambouseraie de Prafrance
- Concoules
- Génolhac
- Porfes
- Alès
- Anduze
- Grotte de Trabuc
- le Mas-Soubeyran
- St Jean-du-Gard
- Museum • Aquarium
- Steam Trains • Clock Tower • Music Museum
- Silk Museum
- St Hippolyte-du-Fort
- C. de la Geryrede
- Vallerauque
- Mont Aigoual
- PARC NATIONAL DES CÉVENNES
- Abime de Bramabiau
- Gorges du Trevezel
- le Vigan
- Museum
- Cirque de Navacelles
- Cirque
- Vissec
- Gorges de la Vis
- CAUSSE DU LARZAC
- LOZÈRE
- Ducal Palace • Crypt • Museum • Cathedral
- Uzès
- Pont du Gard Roman Aquaduct
- Remoulins
- Roman Arena • Museums • Fortress • Roman Temple
- NÎMES
- Sommières
- Castle • Museum • Abbeye de St Roman
- Beaucaire
- St Gilles
- Abbey • Maison Romane
- Arles
- Rhône
- Camargue
- Aigues-Mortes
- Salins du Midi
- le Grau-du-Roi
- Port Camargue
- MONTPELLIER
- HÉRAULT
- Orange
- Roquemaure
- Villeneuve-les-Avignon
- Avignon

Scale: 5miles / 3kms

Compass: N E S W

silkworm moth could incubate in the warmth of their breasts. This technique is not illustrated in the fascinating museum of silk in the town hall.

St Jean-du-Gard, where Robert Louis Stevenson ended his travels and said goodbye to his donkey Modestine (see Lozère Chapter) was also a silk making town. The town's museum, the **Musée des Vallées Cévenols**, housed in a seventeenth-century *auberge*, has a section on the silk industry and other aspects of the agricultural history of the area. Especially interesting is the

Road to Mont Aigoual, Cévennes National Park

Insert: Orchids, Cévennes National Park

section on the chestnut tree – l'Arbe à Pain, the bread tree – so called because the stored nuts made the difference between surviving or not surviving during the harsh Cévennes winter.

Also in the town there is a collection of carriages and cars – 'Le Voyage dans le Temps' – which catalogues the evolution of wheeled transport from the mid-nineteenth century mail coach to modern cars. The **Atlantide Parc** is a collection of aquaria, including an artificial river, filled with mainly tropical fish. St Jean is also one terminus of the Cévennes train (see below).

Close to St Jean are the **Grotte de Trabuc** and **Le Mas Soubeyran**. The *grotte* is the largest cave in the area, with several huge chambers. It has been occupied, on and off, for thousands of years, Neolithic, Roman period and Camisard objects having been found there. Of chief interest inside is an array of small stalagmites called the Cent Mille Soldats, the hundred thousand soldiers, because

of its supposed resemblance to an army.

Within Roland's house is the **Musée du Désert**, *déserts* being the Camisard name for the empty valleys of the Cévennes that protected them so well. Roland's bedroom is as he left it, while the other rooms give an excellent account of the Camisard struggle and the conditions of those who lived and fought in the area at the time.

South of the Le Mas Soubeyran is the **Bambouseraie de Prafrance**, an extraordinary arboretum of bamboo with a 100 acre (40 hectare) bamboo forest. Over 20 different sorts of bamboo thrive here, some with growth rates up to 12 inches (30cm) per day. It is said that some of the plants reach 100ft (30m) high, though 60ft (18m) seems to be the highest on display. There are also more conventional trees and shrubs, if conventional is the correct word to apply to the Californian sequoia and the Egyptian papyrus. The arboretum was the brainchild of

Le Mas Soubeyran

This is the farm where the Camisard leader known simply as Roland was born. The Camisard army never numbered more than 4,000 men, none of them properly trained or equipped, and was, at one time, opposed by a force of 30,000 regular soldiers. The most famous of the Camisard leaders were Jean Cavalier, a baker's apprentice who was 18 when he became a 'general' in the Protestant army, and Roland, a man of whom little is known.

When, after two long years of struggle a stand-off was reached between the Camisards – who could not win – and the Royal army – which could not force a win in the secret valleys of the Cévennes – Cavalier negotiated with the Royalist Marshal de Villiers. It was agreed that all Camisards who wished to leave the area could go in safety. Cavalier went to England and eventually became Governor of Jersey. But Roland could not accept the treaty, seeing it as a betrayal of the Camisard cause and with a few followers he fought on, being killed in 1704, his death signalling the end of the Camisard struggle.

Eugène Mazel who began work here in 1855. It is served by the Cevennes steam train.

South again is **Anduze**, a very picturesque town nestling beneath white tree-studded cliffs beside the River Gard (the name derives from *en deux* – both sides of the river). The town is especially pretty in the old quarter where there is a fine collection of seventeenth-century houses. Nearby is the clock tower, dating from 1320.

The town was the seat of the Duc de Rohan in the early seventeenth century. The Duke was a Huguenot and the castle and walls he built were so strong that when the army of Cardinal Richlieu came here in 1629 to destroy the town the commanders were so intimidated that they attacked nearby Alès instead. Peace was made soon after and the Duke was forced to give up his stronghold, which was promptly destroyed. After the destruction only the clock tower, which pre-dated much of the Duke's work, remained standing. The town is the other terminus of the *train à vapeur des Cévennes*. The SNCF line was closed in 1960, but has been revived by enthusiasts and has regular steam-hauled trains.

 Places to Visit

Cévennes National Park (Gard)

Weather Exhibition
Mont Aigoual
Open: May to September, daily 10am-7pm.
☎ 04 67 82 60 01.

Abîme du Bramabiau (Bellowing Ox Cave)
Nr Col de la Séreyrède
Open: July and August, daily 9am-7pm; Easter to June, September and October, Monday to Saturday 2-6pm, Sunday 10am-12.30pm, 2-6pm. Note that access to the cave may not be possible after prolonged or heavy rain.
☎ 04 67 82 60 78.

Musée Cévenol
1 Rue des Calquieres, Le Vigan
Open: April to October, daily except Tuesday 10am-12noon, 2-6pm; November to March, Wednesday 10am-12noon, 2-6pm.
☎ 04 67 81 06 86.

Silk Museum
Hôtel de Ville, St -Hippolyte-de-Fort
Open: July to August, daily 10am-7pm; April to June, September to November, daily 10am-12.30pm, 2-6.30pm.
☎ 04 66 77 66 47.

Musée des Vallées Cévenoles
St Jean-du-Gard
Open: July and August, daily 10am-7pm; April to June, September and October, daily 10am-12.30pm, 2-7pm; November to March, Tuesday and Thursday 9am-12noon, 2-6pm, Sunday 2-6pm.
☎ 04 66 85 10 48.

Continued over on page 58...

Continued from page 57...

'Le Voyage dans Le Temps'
*Avenue de la Résistance,
St Jean-du-Gard*
Open: July, August, daily 10am-7pm
April to June, September, daily
except Monday and Wednesday
10am-7pm.
☎ 66 85 30 44.

Atlandide Parc
*Avenue de la Résistance,
St Jean-du-Gard*
Open: May to September, daily
9.30am-8pm; October to April,
daily 10am-7pm.
☎ 04 66 85 32 32.

Grottes de Trabuc
Nr St Jean-du-Gard
Open: June to mid-September, daily
9.30am-6.30pm; mid-March to May
and mid-September to mid-October,
daily 9.30am-12noon, 2-6.30pm;
mid-October to November,
Sunday 2-6pm.
☎ 04 66 85 03 28.

Musée du Desert
*Roland's House, near
St Jean-du-Gard*
Open: July and August, daily
9.30am-7pm; September to June,
daily 9.30am-12noon, 2.30-6pm.
☎ 04 66 85 02 72.

Bambouseraie de Prafrance
Nr Anduze
Open: April to September, daily
9.30am-7pm; March and October-
mid-November, 9.30am-6pm.
☎ 04 66 61 70 47.

The Cévennes Steam Train
St Jean-du-Gard to Anduze
Trains run: mid-June to August,
daily; April to mid-June,
daily except Monday;
September, Tuesday, Thursday,
Saturday and Sunday; October,
Saturday and Sunday.
There are four trains daily.
☎ 04 66 85 13 17.

The Cévennes Steam Train

ALÈS AND AROUND

Before visiting Alès, head north to visit the long finger of Gard that runs along the eastern border of the Cévennes National Park. Here Concoules is a charming village, once the capital of the Florentins, a group of armed Catholics, self-styled vigilantes who saw it as their mission to bring Camisards to justice.

Pasteur Statue, Alès

South of Concoules the D315, a narrow, difficult road goes through the hamlet of **Aiguebelle** and then passes the remains of old tile ovens once owned by Nicholas Jouany, a Camisard leader, who made the red tiles for the roofs of Florentin houses in Concoules. The Wars of Religion in France were, indeed, strange conflicts.

To the south is **Génolhac**, another pretty village of red-tiled houses set close to a stream, and **Portes** above which stands the ruins of a fourteenth-century castle. This formidable fortress was occupied and strengthened through to the seventeenth century. During the Revolution it served as a prison, but by the end of the nineteenth century it was ruinous, having, quite literally, been undermined. It is a good example of a medieval/Renaissance château and a fine viewpoint.

Alès is a large, prosperous town that began life as a Celtic village, becoming a market town in medieval times and then a focus for coal mining. Today it is a light industrial town, the old town almost forgotten in the hubbub of commerce, though well remembered in a series of museums.

Two of France's most famous sons spent time in the town, though their stays were quite different. Alphonse Daudet came here as a college servant when his family, strapped for cash, could no longer afford his studies at Lyon. Daudet had a terrible time, at one time contemplating suicide, though the period did give him the inspiration for Le Petit Chose (Little What's His Name) one of his most respected works.

Louis Pasteur's stay could hardly have been more different. Called in to help save the local silk industry from an annual – but increasingly harmful – disease of the mulberry bushes on which the silkworms fed, Pasteur discovered a remedy and was rewarded with a statue – at the edge of the Jardins du Bosquet near Fort Vauban. In it the great man holds aloft some branches while helping a local girl to her feet. The fort behind the statue is an imposing structure, one of the many built to the designs of Maréchal Vauban. Close to the fort is Alès cathedral

which has a Romanesque west front from an earlier building to which an eighteenth-century church has been added.

North-east from Alès is the Château de Rousson, built in the early twelfth century and an excellent example of the period. Further on is the Parc Ornithologique des Isles which has a collection of birds from all parts of the world.

ALÈS TO THE ARDÈCHE GORGE

Continue now into St Ambroix. The Dugas rock, conveniently flat-topped and close to the River Cèze has been occupied from neolithic times. The rock was fortified in the twelfth and fourteenth centuries, but the fortifications were destroyed during the Revolution. To explore, go through the twelfth-century Porte Bertone. Beyond, near the border of Ardèche , the Grotte de la Cocalière has 1,093yd (1,000m) of galleries linking chambers of fine formations and still pools. The cave is unusual in that the visitor exits after a linear walk through the galleries. The cave is one of the longest in France, there being some 30 miles (50km) of explored passageway beyond the show cave.

La Roque-sur-Cèze is charming village – an old bridge over the Cèze, a handful of cypress trees, the old Romanesque church. Go over the bridge and take the clear path to see the fine Cascade du Sautadet, which is a complex series of pools and falls rather than a straight-forward waterfall.

Bagnols-sur-Cèze is very different, a new town built specifically for the workers of the Marcoule

Gorges near St Ambroix

From St Ambroix take the D37 south-eastwards towards **Lussan**, passing the ruins of the Château d'Allègre along the way. At Lussan take the D143. Drive to its end, park and follow the sign for **Portail**. This is the **Gorges de Concluses**. The path follows the Aiguilles stream with views of holes in the stream bed, caves in the rock faces opposite and, eventually, of the Portail (gateway) itself, a natural arch beyond which the stream flows through a tight, exciting gorge. Return is along the same path, the round trip taking about an hour. To the north, the **Gorges de la Cèze** is a less exciting, but picturesque gorge.

Nuclear Centre (on the western bank of the Rhône) having been bolted on, seemingly, to a quaint old town. The oldest part of the old town, in and close to Rue Crémieux, is excellent, as too are town museums. **The Modern Art Museum (Musée Albert André)** – taking up part of the seventeenth-century mansion that is now the Hôtel-de-Ville – houses work by Matisse and Renoir, as well as works by the Albert André of the name, while the **Archaeology Museum (Musée Leon Alegre)** has a good collection of local finds from the Celtic to Roman periods.

North of Bagnols the last town in Gard is **Pont-St Esprit**, named for the magnificent bridge – over 1,000yd (1,000m) long and with 25 solid arches, of which 19 are original – over the Rhône. The towers that once protected each end have long since gone. The first bridge was built by the Brotherhood of the Bridge, set up to provide bridges at places where the local folk could not afford to build. The Brotherhood believed its bridges and workers were protected by the Holy Spirit (St Esprit), hence the name.

The best view of the bridge is from the Terrasse to the south close to the churches of St Saturnin and St Pierre and reached by a huge staircase rising from the Quai de Luynes. Within the town be sure to walk along Rue St Jacques, to the south of the church of St Pierre, where there are a number of excellent old houses, one of which – the Knight's Mansion – dates, in part, from the twelfth century. It houses a museum of sacred art. Close to it is the **Musée Paul Raymond**, housed in the old town hall, which has a collection of work by the early twentieth-century artist Benn.

The Chartreuse de Valbonne

Lying to the north of Bagnols-sur-Cèze, the charterhouse – as monasteries for the Carthusian order were called – was founded in 1203, but rebuilt in the seventeenth century. It is now a hospital. Visitors are allowed in to see the baroque church and cloisters. One monk's cell – the Carthusian monks lived in hermit cells within the main building – has been re-created.

Continued on page 64..

Few visitors to Pont-St Esprit will miss the opportunity of exploring the **Ardéche Gorge**, just over the 'border' from Languedoc, which offers one of the most scenically spectacular drives in France. The gorge, cut by the river of the name, is at its best in the section traversed by the Haute Corniche road, close to the turning to the Aven de Marzal Aven where there are a series of excellent viewpoints (*belvédères*). The most spectacular of these are **Belvédère Sierre de Toure** from where the river is 650ft (200m) vertically below, the **Belvédère de Gaud,** where the view includes the tiny nineteenth century **Château de Gaud**, and the **Belvédère de Gournier** from where a beautiful, winding section of the river is seen. The Gorge is also famous for its caves, with the **Aven de Marzal**, the **Aven d'Orgnac** and **Grotte de la Madeleine**. In addition to the cave, the Aven de Marzal has a museum of caving and a prehistoric zoo with life size dinosaurs, mammoths etc.

Any exploration of the gorge should reach **Pont d'Arc**, a natural rock arch some 120ft (36m) high and 200ft 960m) wide. Originally the river flowed around this limestone snout, but over countless thousands of years it carved its way through the rock creating a shorter path for itself.

Aven de Marzal

*(Cave, Musée de Monde Souterrain
and Prehistoric Zoo)*

Open: July and August, daily 10am-7pm; April to June,
September and October, daily 11am-5pm; March and
November, Sundays and public holidays 10am-12noon, 2-6pm.
☎ 04 75 55 12 45 or 04 75 55 14 82.

Aven d'Orgnac/Musée de Préhistoire

Open: July and August, daily 9.30am-6pm; April to June and
September, daily 9.30am-12noon, 2-6pm; March, October to
mid-November, daily 9.30am-12noon, 2-5pm.
☎ 04 75 38 62 51.

Grotte de la Madeleine

Ardèche Gorge
Open: April to November, daily 10am-6 pm.
☎ 04 75 04 22 20.

BAGNOLS TO VILLENEUVE

South from Bagnols the visitor passes **Roquemaure**, where, in the castle, Pope Clement V died, to reach **Villeneuve-lès-Avignon**. The Rhône here, and for a little way north, is the border between Gard and Bouches-de-Rhône, the first *département* of Provence.

In the late thirteenth century, after the early successes of the Albigensian Crusade, the French crown had acquired the lands of the Counts of Toulouse, while the Holy Roman Empire had gained land on the eastern bank of the Rhône, near Avignon. This land was surrounded by Provence, part of the state controlled by the Count of Avignon who, though giving allegiance to the French king, was an independent ruler. So, when the French king reached the Rhône what he saw across the river was a different country and one that he was not sure he could trust.

When the king, Philippe le Bel – Philip the Fair – arrived there was already a bridge (made famous by the song of dancers who actually dance *sous*, under, rather than *sur*, on, it, using a long-gone 'island' which supported an arch). The bridge was useful, both to commerce and to the military, but to defend the French end the king built a fortified tower. From the top – after climbing the 200 or so steps – there is a marvellous view of Avignon and its Palace of the Popes. In the distance to the north-east is Mont Ventoux.

After the fortification, the King decided to build a new town (a *villeneuve*) between the bridge and Puy Andaon. (The suffix to the name – lès Avignon – means 'close to Avignon'). Interestingly, the king owned the river, the Holy Roman Empire owning the eastern bank. A consequence of this unusual situation (most such boundaries go down the middle of the river) was that when the Rhône waters rose, as they did seasonally, flooding houses in Avignon, the king claimed taxes from the owners of those houses on the grounds that they were now in France!

PONT DU GARD AND UZÈS

From Villeneuve the N100 takes the visitor towards Pont du Gard, passing through **Remoulins**, important for fruit growing. In spring, when the trees are in blossom, this area is very beautiful. Beyond is **Pont du Gard**.

The Roman aqueduct of Pont du Gard almost defies superlatives: it is said to be the third most visited site in France (after the Eiffel Tower and Versailles); it is the highest of all Roman aqueducts, at 160ft (48m) above the river; and only Segovia can compete with it for state of preservation. Yet these are bare facts. The aqueduct is more than a piece of engineering, it is a work of art. It was built in 19BC when the fresh water supply of Roman Nîmes was failing to meet demand. Having discovered an excellent new source of water near Uzès, the Romans piped it the 30 miles (50km) down a channel engineered to drop $1/_{40}$ inch every yard (1mm every 100cm). They bored tunnels to take the water through hills that were inconveniently in the way, but the greatest challenge was crossing the River Gard (or Gardon).

In addition to the **Tour Phillippe-le-Bel Villeneuve** has several fine visitor sites. During the time of the Avignon Popes life in Avignon grew progressively more decadent and obnoxious, and many Cardinals chose to have palaces built in Villeneuve. Most were destroyed during the Revolution, but that of Cardinal Pierre-de-Luxembourg in Rue de la République, fourteenth-century and superbly restored, houses a museum of religious art. Two pieces here, a fourteenth-century Virgin carved from an elephant's trunk and the mid-fifteenth century Coronation of the Virgin by Enguerrand Quarton, are masterpieces.

Philip the Fair's Tower

Open: April to September, daily 10am-12.30pm, 3-7.30pm;
October to January, March, daily except Monday 10am-12noon, 2-5.30pm.
☎ 04 90 27 49 68.

Musée Cardinal Pierre-de-Luxembourg

Rue de la République
Open: April to September, daily except Monday 10am-12.30pm, 3-7pm;
October to January, March, daily except Monday 10am-12noon, 2-5.30pm.
☎ 04 90 27 49 66.

Puy Andaon once had a natural moat, an arm of the Rhône going around it, so it was natural that it was fortified. The present fortifications, **Fort André**, date from the late fourteenth century and are a superb example of the period. Indeed, many experts claim that the fortified gate is *the* finest example of the period. Inside there are the remains of an old chapel and some of the medieval houses that once stood inside the walls, and of the abbey, Abbaye St André, that stood over the remains of St Casarie. The abbey has fine, Italianate gardens.

Fort St André

Open: April to September, daily 10am-12.30pm, 2-6pm; October to March, daily except Tuesday 10am-12noon, 2-5pm.
☎ 04 90 25 45 35.

Abbaye St André

Fort St André
Open: April to September, daily except Monday 10am-12.30pm, 2-6pm; October to March, daily except Tuesday 10am-12noon, 2.30-5pm.
☎ 04 90 25 55 95.

Close to the west wall of the fort is the **Chartreuse du Val de Bénédiction** which dates from 1352 when the head of the Carthusian Order was elected Pope, but refused the office out of humility. The new vote elected Innocent VI who gave his palace to the order as a new charterhouse. During the Revolution, the last monks were thrown out and the building was used by squatters and bandits. Today it has been restored to its original calm and is a focus for culture. The church houses the tomb of Pope Innocent VI.

Chartreuse du Val de Bénédiction

Open: All year, daily 9am-6.30pm (5.30pm October to March).
☎ 04 90 15 24 24.

The aqueduct was, of course, built by hand, a giant treadmill acting as a crane to lift blocks of dressed stone weighing up to 6 tons (6.1 tonnes) into position. The arches of the triple span aqueduct were built individually so that the structure could flex in the event of flooding or ground subsidence. The final span carries the water channel, a square channel formed of stone blocks, the joints sealed with iron.

When built the aqueduct carried 44 million gallons (200 million litres) of water each day to Nîmes, about 88 gallons (400 litres) for each resident of the Roman city. The water channel was covered, some of the covering slabs still being in position. The visitor who clambers up the side of the Pont can see these – and walk along them if they are so inclined. The view is stupendous, but a head for heights is needed, as is a calm day.

The aqueduct had one drawback – lime deposits built up on the channel stones requiring constant maintenance. Once this stopped in the fourth century the water supply went into decline. By the ninth century water had stopped flowing and the whole watercourse was being pirated for building stone. Napoleon III rebuilt the Pont in the nineteenth century and despite the medieval hacking to create a packhorse bridge, by widening the original road, it remains a joy. Interestingly, at St Bonnet-du-Gard part of the church was built with the lime deposit excavated from the water channel, this making a superb building stone.

The water that ran over the Pont du Gard came from **Uzès**, a quite beautiful city that seems to have been kidnapped from Renaissance Tuscany and hidden in Languedoc.

The city's focal point is the Duché, the Ducal Palace, in whose courtyard stands the fourteenth-century Viscounty Tower (with an octagonal turret) and the eleventh-century Bermonde Tower (the square keep with the delightful

Pont du Gard

Above: Tour Fenestrelle
Left: Stone detail, Ducal Palace
Below: Ducal Palace, Uzés

History of Uzès

The Dukes of Uzès claimed descent from Charlemagne and rose to be the first Dukes of the realm in the mid-seventeenth century. Sadly the town was Huguenot and its medieval walls were destroyed by Richelieu. The boulevards of Gambette, Gide, Victor-Hugo and Le Portalet now follow the route of the old walls. Inside these roads many of the houses date from the seventeenth and eighteenth centuries when the town grew prosperous on the manufacture of silk and linen, but enough medieval buildings remain to convince the visitor that the Dukes had a strong link to northern Italy.

crenellations). The Bermonde can be climbed for a fine view over the town. The Palace has a fine Renaissance façade, behind which are richly decorated rooms with fine furniture.

Close to the Palace are the excellent eighteenth-century Hôtel-de-Ville and the Crypte, a fourth-century Christian sanctuary and later baptistery. From the crypt, walk along Rue Boucairie and Rue Rafin, passing the Hôtel des Monnaies, the Duchy's mint in medieval times. Continuing, a complex of buildings is reached. To the left is the Hôtel du Baron de Castille, a colonnaded eighteenth-century mansion and the old bishop's palace. Part of the building houses the city museum, with collections on local history and folklore, furniture and art and a collection of memorabilia of André Gide, a member of an important local family, who won the Nobel Prize for Literature in 1947.

Next to the old palace is the Cathedral of St Théodorit, an interesting seventeenth-century building which replaced an original destroyed during the Wars of Religion. All that remains of the original cathedral is the Tour Fenestrelle beside it. This tower six floors high – named for its array of double windows – is twelfth-century and resembles the famous tower in Pisa.

Across from the tower is the Promenade Jean-Racine, a fine walk with lovely views. The names commemorate the stay in the city of Jean Racine, the seventeenth-century playwright and poet. Of Uzès he later wrote:

Goodbye, city of Uzés,
city of good cheer
Where twenty innkeepers thrive,
while one bookseller dies.

Finally, be sure to see the Place aux Herbes, a magnificent market square with covered arcades. Close by is another tower, the Tour de l'Horloge, the twelfth-century clock tower. It was in this part of Uzés, where the old houses are the best preserved, that the Gerald Depardieu film Cyrano de Bergerac was filmed.

To the south-west of Uzés, between the villages of Aureillac and Arpillargues, at the **Moulin de Chalier** the **Musée 1900s** has a collection of early twentieth-century vehicles – cars, motor cycles, bicycles and trains – while the **Musée de Train et du Jouet** has a miniature railway, toy collection and models of the local places of interest. Finally, those with an interest in horses could visit the **French National Stud** which lies beside the road to Alès.

East of Alès

Grotte de la Cocalière

Nr St Ambroix
Open: July and August, daily 10am-
6pm; April to June, September and
October, daily 10am-12noon, 2-5pm.
☎ 04 66 24 01 57.

Musée d'Art Moderne Albert-André

Place Mallet, Bagnols-sur-Cèze
Open: March-January, daily except
Monday 10am-12noon, 3-7pm
(2-6pm September to June).
☎ 04 66 50 50 56.

Musée d'Archéologie Léon Alègre

*Maison Jourdan, 24 Avenue Paul
Langevin, Bagnols-sur to Cèze*
Open: March-January, Thursday to
Saturday 10am-12noon, 3-7pm
(2-6pm September to June).
☎ 04 66 89 74 00.

The Chartreuse de Valbonne

North of Bagnols-sur-Cèze
Open: All year, Monday to Saturday
9am-12noon, 1.30-5.30pm, Sunday
2-7pm. In July and August,
open daily 10am-1pm, 2-7pm.
☎ 04 66 90 41 24.

Musée d'Art Sacré du Gard

*Maison des Chevaliers,
2 Rue St-Jacques, Pont-St Esprit*
Open: mid-June to mid-September,
daily except Monday 10am-12noon,
3-7pm (2-6pm mid-September
to mid-June).
☎ 04 66 39 17 61.

Musée Paul Raymond

*Place de l'Ancienne Mairie,
Pont-St Esprit*
Open: July to September, daily

except Monday 10am-12noon,
3-7pm; October to January, March
to June, Wednesday, Thursday and
Sunday 10am-12noon, 2-6pm.
☎ 04 66 39 09 98 .

Ducal Palace

Uzès
Open: July to mid-September,
daily 10am-6.30pm; October to June,
daily 10am-12noon, 2-6pm.
☎ 04 66 22 18 96.

Crypte

Uzès
Open: During tours of the town only.
Contact the Tourist Information
Office, Avenue de la Libération,
☎ 04 66 22 68 88.

Musée Georges-Borias (Town Museum)

*Ancien Évêché (Old Bishop's Palace),
Uzès*
Open: All year except January, daily
except Monday 3-6pm (2-5pm in
November and December).
☎ 04 66 22 40 23.

Musée 1900s/Musée du Train et du Jouet

*Moulin de Chalier, Aureillac/
Arpaillargues*
Open: July and August, daily 9am-
7pm; September to June, daily
except Monday 9am-12noon, 2-7pm.
☎ 04 66 22 58 64.

French National Stud

Route d'Alès, Uzès
Open: daily except Sunday 2-5pm.
☎ 04 66 22 68 88.

The Arena at Nîmes is the best preserved Roman amphitheatre in the world, though not the largest, and is magnificent both for its architecture and its engineering. It owes its existence to its having been used as a fortress after the Romans left France and its use as a village in medieval times. Then, up to 2,000 people lived in an array of ramshackle houses inside the walls. When excavated 25ft (8m) of rubble and rubbish had to be dug out – but the muck had preserved it.

The Arena is an oval 436ft x 331ft (133m x 101m) created of 60 arcades each 68ft (21m) high. It could hold 24,000 people and the entrances/exits were so well constructed that it is estimated that it could be emptied in just a few minutes. The spectators in Roman times watched the usual array of savage games – the central area was even made watertight so that sea battles could take place – protected from the sun by a movable awning. Today the Arena is still in use, most particularly for bullfights. Both *corridas*, Spanish fighting ending with a kill, and *cocardes*, Provençal style where the *razeteur* attempts to remove a rosette (*cocardo*) from between the bulls horns.

Arena

Open: June to September, daily 9am-6.30pm;
October to May, daily 9am-12noon, 2-5pm.
Closed on the day of a bullfight or show.
☎ 04 66 76 72 77.

The Maison Carrée is the best preserved Roman temple in existence, its preservation due to its usefulness as, at various times, stable, bordello, town hall.... It was built about 30BC and was probably dedicated to the Capitoline Trinity (Juno, Minerva and Jupiter) as it was known locally as the Capitol until it acquired its present name in the sixteenth century.

Maison Carrée means 'square house' which implies a woeful ignorance of geometry (though it has been suggested that *carré* meant oblong at one time). With its Corinthian columns, pediments and friezes the temple shows a clear Greek influence and is a masterpiece. Within the *cella* (the room that held

Roman Amphitheatre, Nimes

the statue of the god to whom the temple was dedicated) temporary exhibitions are held.

Maison Carrée

Open: June to September, daily 9am-12noon, 2.30-7pm;
October to May, daily 9am-12.30pm, 2-6pm.
☎ 04 66 36 26 76.

In the Jardin de la Fontaine – a beautiful garden laid out in the eighteenth century and worth visiting for its trees and terraces – are the Temple of Diana and the Tour Magne. Of the Temple, built around 150AD, very little is known. It is not clear if it was actually a temple and certainly not clear it was ever dedicated to Diana. Sadly it has not withstood the tests of time as well as other more famous remains, suffering partial demolition during the Wars of Religion. The Tour Magne may pre-date the Romans, though they undoubtedly refurbished it and incorporated it into their ramparts.

To the east of the Jardin de la Fontaine is a seventeenth-century fortress at the base of which is the Castellum, a water tower that received and distributed the water from the Uzès aqueduct. Distribution was through a series of ten lead pipes.

Magne Tower

Open: June to September, daily 9am-7pm; October to May, daily 9am-5pm.
☎ 04 66 67 65 56.

NÎMES

South of Uzés is Nîmes, its name deriving from Nemausus, the god of the spring of freshwater that surfaces in the Jardin de la Fontaine, in the north-west part of the present town. The spring naturally attracted the Romans when they arrived in southern France and Nîmes was soon a thriving Roman city. The Romans built the aqueduct from Uzès when the spring failed to support the rising population, and they also built the two wonders of the city – the Arena and Maison Carrée.

The fortress above the Castellum was built in 1687 two years after Louis XIV had revoked the Edict of Nantes. Nîmes had been staunchly Protestant throughout the Wars of Religion, the local battles culminating with the Michelade (on 29 September 1567) when 200 Catholic priests and nuns were massacred. After a further century of unrest, the fortress was built to keep an eye on a sullen population.

• THE MUSEUMS OF NÎMES •

Opposite the Maison Carrée is the **Carré d'Art**, designed by Norman Foster to house a museum of contemporary art.

Carré d'Art

Open: All year, daily except Monday 10am-6pm.
☎ 04 66 76 35 70.

In Boulevard Amiral Courbet an old Jesuit College has been converted into the **Musée Archéologique** on the ground floor (with items from the town's pre-Roman and Roman eras and from other countries) and the **Musée d'Histoire Naturelle** (on the first floor) with a collection that includes some ethnographic exhibits.

Musée d'Archéologie

Open: All year, daily except Monday 11am-6pm.
☎ 04 66 67 25 57.

Muséum d'Histoire Naturelle

Open: All year, daily except Monday 11am-6pm.
☎ 04 66 67 39 21.

Blue denim

The peace that ensued did allow the town to prosper again, especially as a result of a heavy blue serge cloth that became known as denim (from de Nîmes). In 1848 a Californian called Levi Strauss used the cloth, and a few rivets, to make wear-resistant trousers for Gold Rush miners. And the rest, as they say, is history.

Staying with the famous, a Nîmes man born in 1650 is credited (if that is the word) with introducing tobacco to France. His name was Jean Nicot, and in his name the drug isolated from the tobacco leaf was called nicotine. A more artistic connection is passed by the visitor who takes Boulevard Gambetta between the Jardin de la Fontaine and Porte d'Auguste. No. 20 is the birthplace of the nineteenth-century writer Alphonse Daudet.

A short distance away, beside the cathedral (an eleventh-century foundation but virtually rebuilt in the nineteenth century) is the **Musée de Vieux Nîmes**. The museum occupies the ground floor of the old bishop's palace and has a collection of locally made furnishings from the seventeenth and eighteenth centuries.

Musée de Vieux-Nîmes

Open: All year, daily except Monday 11am-6pm.
☎ 04 66 36 00 64.

The **Musée des Beaux-Arts** in Rue Cité-Foule has a collection of fifteenth-nineteenth century paintings, chiefly by French artists, but including Dutch and Italian works.

Musée des Beaux-Arts

Open: All year daily, except Monday 11am-6pm.
☎ 04 66 67 38 21.

Finally, close to the Arena, **Galerie Taurine** holds paintings, posters and costumes relating to bullfighting.

Galerie Taurine

Open: Whit Sunday to September, daily except Monday 11am-6pm.
☎ 04 66 76 74 49.

BEAUCAIRE TO THE COAST

To the east of Nîmes is Beaucaire. When the Rhône was the border between France and the Holy Roman Empire, the guardians of the castles of Beaucaire and Tarascon glared at each other across the river and kept watch for the *tarasque*. This legendary monster was banished to the river by Ste Marthe of the Camargue, after it had made a nuisance of itself by eating local children.

Beaucaire

Time has served Beaucaire and its fortress poorly. The castle ruin is picturesque, though, and from the top of the walls near the Tour Polygonale (named for its unusual shape) the view to Tarascon is superb. Within the castle there is a small Romanesque chapel and the Musée Auguste-Jacquet, which houses a collection of lapidary and finds from the Gallo-Roman period.

Elsewhere in the town, be sure to see the church of Notre-Dame des Pommiers, a fine building that retains its Romanesque qualities despite extensive rebuilding in the eighteenth century. Close by (at 23 Rue de la République) is the Maison des Cariatides, a seventeenth-century house with a beautiful, carved façade that is named for the caryat-

ids to the sides of the porch. It is sad that so fine a façade has been so neglected, as, indeed, has the rest of this once elegant street.

A little way north of Beaucaire is the Abbaye de St Roman. The abbey has an unsettled history, having been built in the twelfth century, but abandoned in the sixteenth century and converted into a castle. The site has now been excavated and partially restored. The abbey was set on a limestone outcrop from where there are beautiful views to Avignon, Mont Ventoux and the Luberon Hills of Provence. Southwest of Beaucaire is St Gilles.

Of the abbey little remains, much having been destroyed by the Huguenots who threw the monks down the abbey's well. The west face, with

St Gilles

The saint was born in eighth century Greece and journeyed from there to Provence by raft to preach the gospel. Landing near the Camargue he was befriended by a local lord whom he saved from death by plucking a huntsman's arrow out of mid-air. The man founded an abbey at the site of the miracle. The Pope, hearing of the miracle, summoned Gilles to Rome and presented him with a pair of doors for the abbey. To the Pope's consternation Giles threw them into the Tiber, but they miraculously floated to the Camargue and up the Petit Rhône to the abbey. It may have been outside these doors that Raymond VI, Count of Toulouse murdered a Papal Legate on 15 January 1208, the killing being the trigger for the Albigensian Crusade.

its friezes and reliefs telling the story of Christ, but with some Old Testament episodes, is thought by many to be the finest Romanesque sculpture in France. Within the crypt lies the tomb of St Gilles: it was once the site of one of the greatest pilgrimages in France. Nearby, the Vis de St Gilles, a spiral staircase still draws gasps of admiration from stonemasons so fine is the quality of its jointing.

Elsewhere in the village, be sure to visit the **Maison Romane**, the Romanesque House. This was the birthplace of Guy Foulque, elected Pope Clement IV in 1265. Inside are items excavated from the abbey church, a museum of local birds and a collection of old craft tools.

From St Gilles to **Aigues-Mortes** the visitor follows the western edge of the **Camargue**, that legendary land of white horses, black bulls and flamingoes. It is a place at once fascinating, especially for the bird-watcher and the romantic, and infuriating, as it is very difficult to find anywhere that is the essential Camargue. Those who wish to try should go to the Information Centre at **Ginès**, the **Camargue Museum at Mas du Pont de Rousty**, the **Pont de Gau Bird Sanctuary** or, and perhaps best of all, try a boat trip on the Petit Rhône from **Stes-Maries-de-la-Mer**.

Crusade of Louis IX

When, in the early thirteenth century Louis IX decided to set out on a Crusade he needed a Mediterranean port to shorten the journey. Marseilles would have been ideal, of course, but it lay on the 'foreign' side of the Rhône. So the King built his own port, choosing a tiny fishing village in the western Camargue as his starting point. The village lay among the dead waters of the Camargue's saltmarshes, that fact giving the new port its name – Aigues-Mortes.

On 28 August 1248, Louis' fleet set sail from his new port. There were 1,500 ships carrying 35,000 men, together with horses and supplies. The Seventh Crusade was a splendid affair, but it was not a success. Louis was captured in 1250, ransomed and returned to France in 1254. The Crusade's failure haunted him and by 1270 he was ready to try again. This time the fleet sailed east, not west, and landed in Tunis, for reasons not wholly understood. There, Louis died of fever, as did his son and a large part of his army.

What Louis built is an almost perfect walled town, the streets laid out on a grid, the walls protected by towers and gates. The ramparts can – and should – be walked, the wall exploring the view of the town from all angles and passing all the towers and gates. The **Wick Tower** (Tour de la Mèche) on the northern wall is named for a lantern that hung there at all times not, as might be supposed, to act as a beacon for ships or voyagers, but to provide a flame for cannons during battle.

The **Burgundian Tower** (Tour des Bourguignons) on the western corner is named for an incident during the Hundred Years War. The Burgundians had captured the town but were besieged by a Gascon army. Some Gascons secretly gained access to the town, opened the gates to their colleagues and the Burgundians were slaughtered. So many corpses were there that time was needed for burials to be arranged and carried out, so the Burgundians' corpses were thrown into the bottom of the tower and covered in salt to preserve them.

The largest tower is the **Tour de Constance**. It stands 130ft (40m) high, is 72ft (22m) in diameter and has walls 20ft (6m) thick. Inside are reminders of medieval life, including graffiti carved by Huguenot prisoners, two of whom escaped in true legendary fashion, by climbing down knotted sheets. From the top of the tower there is the very best view of the town.

Close to Aigues-Mortes is **Les Salins du Midi**, a saltmarsh that has for centuries been used for the production of salt. The process is an interesting one, and is explained to visitors, but the end product does not attract tasters in the way that visits to the nearby **Caves de Listel** (the cellars of the Domaine de Jarras) do.

It would be interesting to know what the Crusader King, Louis IX, would think of **Port-Camargue**, the purpose-built marina beside the old fishing village of **Le Grau-du-Roi**. The marina is a marvel of both engineering and of organization, the latter the more so because the 4,000 berths are divided between short-term and winter berths and are connected by seemingly endless walkways and water channels. Le Grau, the older port, seems very tame by comparison, but does have a definite charm.

North of Aigues-Mortes is the **Château de Teillan**. The château, which is set in fine parkland, began life as a priory, but was sold and extended in the seventeenth century. The watchtower offers a view of the Camargue and Aigues-Mortes, and into Hérault. There is also a dovecote with 1,500 nest sites reached by a revolving ladder.

Perrier water

North again is the Source Perrier. The spring that produces the famous mineral water creates an underground lake. Escaping gas is captured and used to re-gasify the water, which is bottled on site. Visitors are allowed in (guided tours only) to watch as some of the 800 million bottles sold annually are filled.

Finally, head westwards to **Sommières**. Here the River Vidourle is crossed by **Pont Romain**, although in truth little remains of the original Roman bridge. Within the town there is a superb pair of arcaded markets looked over by the rem-nants of an old castle. During the Revolution this was used as a prison for ladies who, the Revolutionary leaders said, were rendering their men useless as idealistic soldiers by offering them, shall we say, more earthly pleasures.

Places to Visit

Beaucalre to the Coast

Castle/ Musée Auguste-Jacquet

Beaucaire
Open: April to September, daily except Tuesday 10am-12noon, 2.15-6.45pm (opens at 10.15am October to March).
☎ 04 66 59 47 61.

Abbaye de St Roman

Nr Beaucaire
Open: April to September, daily 10am-6pm (6.30pm in July and August); October to March, Saturday and Sunday 2-5pm.
☎ 04 66 59 52 26.

St Gilles Abbey

Open: All year, daily except Sundays and public holidays 9am-12noon, 2-5pm (3-7pm in July and August, 2-6pm in June and September).
☎ 04 66 87 41 31.

Maison Romane

St Gilles
Open: July and August, daily except Sunday 9am-12noon, 3-7pm; September to June, daily except Sunday 9am-12noon, 2-5pm.
☎ 04 66 87 40 42.

Constance Tower/ Town Walls

Aigues-Mortes
June to September, daily 9.30am-7.30pm (6.30pm in September); October to May, daily 9.30am-12.30pm, 2-5pm (6pm in April and May).
☎ 04 66 53 61 55.

Les Salins du Midi

Nr Aigues-Mortes
Open: July and August, guided tours on Wednesday and Friday (organised by the Aigues-Mortes Tourist Information Office, ☎ 04 66 53 77 00 or at the site ☎ 04 66 53 85 20.

Caves de Listel

Nr Aigues-Mortes
Open: Easter to October, daily 10am-6.30pm; November to Easter, Monday-Friday 9am-11.30pm, 2-5.30pm.
☎ 04 66 51 17 00.

Château de Teillan

Nr Marsillargues
Open: mid-June to mid-September, daily except Monday 2-6pm.
☎ 04 66 88 02 38.

Source Perrier

Nr Nîmes
Open: July and August, Monday to Friday 9am-7pm, Saturday and Sunday 9.30am-7pm; September to June, Monday to Friday 9am-6pm, Saturday and Sunday 1-7pm.
☎ 04 66 87 61 01.

3

Lozère

Although part of Languedoc, Lozère is quite distinct from the sea-lapped *départements* to the south. Yet it is equally distinct from the volcanic landscape of the Auvergne to the north. The northern end of the *département* suggests that after creating the peaks of the Massif Central, but before producing the wondrous country of clear light to the south, nature paused for breath.

The northern *département* is pleasant, but hardly inspiring country, a land of gentle hills and streams. But as an overall impression of Lozère, the north gives a quite mistaken view. Southwards the country changes into some of the most dramatic in France: the high limestone plateaux of the Causses, the Gorges du Tarn and the magnificent country of the Cévennes, so good, and so unique that it has been granted the status of a National Park.

THE NORTHERN AREA

The north of Lozère is now waking up to its potential as a visitor area. Though scenically unable to compete with the south, it has peace and tranquillity and huge open spaces. Already there are excellent hotels and restaurants, set up to cater for those who want a less hurried tour. Close to Baraque-de-Bouviers, hardly even a hamlet, on the D5 which links Serverette and Grandrieu, there is an excellent viewpoint of the Monts de la Margeride, the upland mass that runs like an upturned boat southwards from Cantal/Haute Loire.

Close by is **Le Malzieu**, a still-walled medieval town. The walls, 25-35ft (8-10m) high, with their towers and gates, are the main attraction, though the town within – laid out on a geometric pattern – is also worthwhile. Close to Le Malzieu **is St Alban-sur-Limagnole**, a village on the pilgrimage route to Santiago de Compostela – note the shells on the capitals of the church – though the village name derives from the first British saint. The village's castle, built in the mid-thirteenth century – is now part of a psychiatric unit, but can still be visited.

Southwards from Le Malzieu the visitor climbs up the Gévaudan plateau and reaches the **Parc de Gévaudan**. Here European wolves, supplemented by animals from Canada and Mongolia roam a large forest park. The park is a curious echo of the legend of the Beast of Gévaudan.

To the west of the wolf park is the **Château de Baume**, built in the latter half of the seventeenth century of a somewhat leaden-looking granite which belies an elegant interior.

Nasbinals, a village close to the point where Lozère, Cantal and

The Beast of Gévaudan

Gévaudan is a plateau lying below La Margeride which, for three years between 1764 and 1767, was terrorized by an unknown killer. The first killing took place on 3 July 1764, after which many other people – chiefly children and young woman – died. Many of the victims (the exact number is not known, but it seems to have been 40-60, at least) were eaten. Tales of a were-wolf were rife, particularly as the beast was seen on at least a dozen occasions. The witnesses claimed the beast was wolf-like, but usually walked on its hind-legs. Many said it made human gestures and was definitely a man, perhaps dressed in an animal skin. Finally, on 19 June 1767 a local hunter, Jean Chastel, shot a huge wolf and the killings ceased. But was the wolf the real culprit?

Chastel's family was an odd one. His father was known to practise black magic, his brother was a half-crazed youth who roamed the woods with a pack of manic dogs. Many believed that the younger boy, Antoine, was the killer and had been silenced by the family, the dead wolf being a convenient cover up. The truth will never be known.

Aveyron meet is a starting point for walking, particularly in Aubrac Forest over the border in Aveyron. The village's little church, built in Romanesque style in the twelfth century, is also worth visiting.

South of Nasbinals are the **Monts d'Aubrac**, most of which lie in Aveyron. This is less wooded country, where the transhumance (the twice yearly migration of the herds and people, to and from the high pastures) of the cow herds still takes place, in a limited way. The processions became, in part, a religious festival, the cows, decked out in ribbons and bouquets, sometimes accompanied by a statue of the Virgin that was carried to, or from, an upland chapel. Today's visitor will not see a real transhumance, such movements as do take place now usually being by lorry, but occasion-ally as part of a festival, flower-bedecked cows, sheep and goats are moved.

To explore the Lozère Aubrac take the D52 (turn right off the D900 south of Nasbinals. The **Grotte et Cascade de Déroc** are soon passed, a small cave and pretty waterfall reached with a walk of about 15 minutes from a marked lay-by. Further on, the road crosses the Col de Bonnecombe and then descends past several fine viewpoints to reach **Le Monastier**, which has a fine eleventh-century church, and **Marvejols**, a pretty place with several fine old gates remaining from the medieval town walls. On the Porte du Soub-eyran there is an inscription noting that the town was built by Henri IV. A statue of the king stands close by: if it is an exact likeness Henri was in very poor health. If it is not, it is

• BERTRAND DU GUESCLIN •

Guesclin was the finest French general of the Hundred Years War, becoming Constable of France in 1370. His strategy was to avoid set piece battles with the English, preferring a stratagem that confused the opposition and led to superior positions. Bertrand was brave to the point of foolhardiness, as a result of which he was twice captured by the English. On each occasion he was ransomed back to France, which seems to say a great deal about the greed and incompetence of the English generals. On the second occasion the ransom was 40,000 francs, a huge sum.

In 1380 du Guesclin was at Châteauneuf attempting to wrest this area of central France back from the English who had been in possession of it for 10 years. On a summer's day in July he drank water from a cold spring. The effect of the icy water on him was dramatic: whether he contracted pneumonia or some other ailment is not known, but within hours he was dead. His dying request was that he be buried in Dinan, in Brittany, so a carriage was procured and a small procession set off.

By the time the cortege had reached Le Puy-en-Velay it became apparent that du Guesclin's body would not make it to Brittany without drastic action. So at Le Puy the body was drawn, the entrails being placed in a shrine in the church, and then embalmed. The cortege moved on, but by Montferrand it had become clear that the embalming had failed. The heart was removed and the flesh boiled from the bones. The flesh was cremated, the ashes interred in the church and the cortege moved on.

Next, at Le Mans, soldiers arrived from the king in Paris. They demanded the bones, which were taken off for burial in the capital. Finally, the heart was interred at Dinan. This gruesome tale meant that du Guesclin was buried in four separate French churches. That number is now three, the church at Montferrand having been destroyed by Revolutionaries in 1793, the ashes dispersed.

as well the artist and the king did not meet face to face.

In the north-east of the *département*, on the border with Ardéche, is **Langogne**, a town set in the val-ley of the River Allier. The town is close to the southern tip of the huge Naussac lake created, in part, to control water flow in the Allier, but which is also popular with water

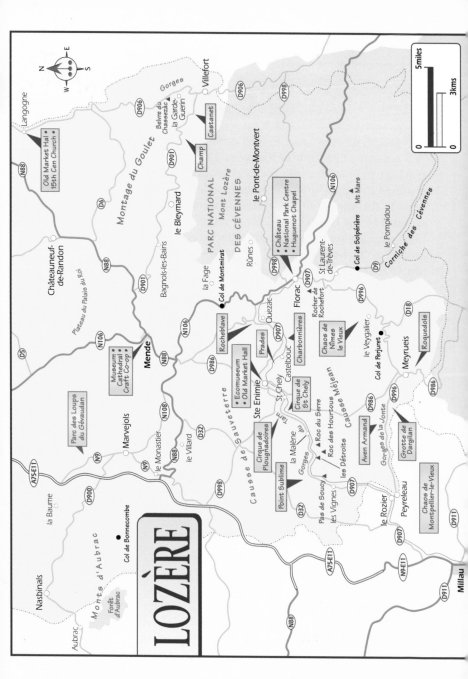

LOZÈRE

sports enthusiasts. Within the town there is a fine eighteenth-century market hall, and a fifteenth-century church with delightful sculpted capitals.

Heading south from Langogne the visitor soon reaches **Châteauneuf-de-Randon** one of the prettiest villages in France. France has a system of defining exquisite villages so that

Above: Mende

Below: Lake near Villefort

the visitor need only look at the approved list to discover those which are worth visiting. At first glance this seems a little curious – does anyone really need a list to be able to work out whether a village is picturesque? However, for the visitor the list is invaluable though there will always be those that complain over the inclusion or exclusion of a particular village.

With Châteauneuf there would be no dissent. The village is set on a high, rocky ridge. At its highest point, close to the old château – known as the new castle (hence the village name) as an earlier one had been destroyed during prolonged battles with the English – a panorama dial picks out the vital points of the view. The strategic position this view implies is the reason Châteauneuf was so important during the campaigns of the late fourteenth century. In the village square there is a fine bronze statue of Bertrand du Guesclin.

MENDE

South of Châteauneuf the N88 goes through a gap between the Plateau du Palais du Roi and the Montagne du Goulet to reach the Lot Valley and **Mende**. Mende is the main city of Lozère, yet it looks more like a market town (which it is) than a *départemental* capital. The town owes its origins to St Privat who fled to a cell here when barbarians invaded central France in the third century. St Privat was found and murdered, his body being buried in a tomb that was, later, a site of pilgrimage. Later still, when the cathedral was begun in the fourteenth century, the saint's tomb was incorporated as a crypt, one of the oldest crypts in France.

Much of the cathedral was built with money donated by Pope Urban V, the Lozère-born Guillaume de Grimoard. It is a solid, rather than elegant, Gothic building which took many years to build and many more to restore after being partially destroyed by the Huguenots in 1579. The Huguenots destroyed the cathedral's great bell – one of the biggest in France: now only the clapper remains. Also inside is a very old (probably eleventh-century) Black Virgin. Such dark statues are a feature of central France, and the Auvergne in particular, and were carved of very dark wood which, with time, became almost black. The Mende statue is of Lebanon cedar and is thought to have been brought back from a Crusade. When it was revealed that the statue contained strands of the Virgin Mary's hair and of the True Cross, Mende's importance increased substantially.

Elsewhere, Mende is a delightful mix of ancient street and modern amenity. The Lot is crossed by Pont Notre-Dame, a picturesque thirteenth-century stone bridge. The **Musée Ignon-Fabre** has items on the history and folklore of the area. The town also has an excellent craft co-operative at 4 Rue de l'Ange, between the cathedral and the museum.

MENDE TO VILLEFORT

To the east of Mende the D901 follows the Lot almost all the way back to its source on the southern flank of the **Montagne du Goulet**. It then crosses the **Col des Tribes** and follows the River Allier down to the lake at Villefort. This is a beautiful, if occasionally trying, road, with superb scenery to both sides and a number of interesting stops along the way.

Bagnols-les-Bains is an old spa – at least as old as the Romans – which claims maximum benefit for those suffering from rheumatic-based conditions. Further on is **Le Bleymard** its old houses, many still roofed with the cleaved stones known locally as *lauzes*, grouped around a charming thirteenth-century church. From close to the village the D901 crosses the Col des Tribes (3,709ft – 1,131m) and descends towards Villefort and its lake.

The road passes close to the towers of the **Château de Champ**, to the right, then reaches the **Château de Castanet**. This square granite castle, with its oddly-roofed corner towers, was built in the late sixteenth century. Inside, its rooms are in Renaissance style and are used for summer exhibitions. Strangely, whereas the flooding of valleys is usually deplored, the creation of the Villefort Lake saved Castanet from being demolished, the land beneath it no longer being of value.

Villefort is a quiet, elegant little town used by many visitors as a base for exploring the Cévennes National Park (there is a Park Information Centre in the town) or as a base for those sampling the delights of the lake. To the north is **La Garde-Guérin**.

La Garde-Guérin

In Roman times the only route through the high land of Mont Lozère was that now taken by the D906. The Romans built a road along that route, the Chemin de Régordane, but when they left the area the route lost its police force. Increasingly it was patrolled by highwaymen preying on people who had no choice but to use it. Chief of these were the muleteers who hauled salt from Aigues-Mortes, at the edge of the Camargue, into central France. On their return journey the men had pockets jangling with coins and were easy targets.

Eventually the Bishop of Mende decided that enough was enough and built the fortified village of La Garde-Guérin. He built a castle and a series of well-defended houses, in each of which a knight was installed. The knight's job was to ride with any anyone using the road, for a fee, and to protect him from attack. Many of the knights' houses still stand: they are formidable and granite built, even to the window mullions, and grouped around the remnants of the old castle. The old tower can be climbed, but needs a bold approach and a steady head. From the top there is a fine view of the village and, in the opposite direction, the impressive Gorges du Chassezac.

Northern Lozère

Parc à Loups du Gévaudan (Wolf Park)

Nr Marvejols
Open: June to September, daily
10am-6 pm; October to December
and February to May,
daily 10am-4.30pm.
☎ 04 66 32 09 22.

Château de Baume

Nr Marvejols
Open: mid-June to mid-September,
daily 10am-12noon, 2-6pm;
mid-September to mid-June,
daily except Tuesday 2-5pm
but by appointment only.
☎ 04 66 32 51 59.

Musée Ignon-Fabre

Mende
Closed for restoration at the
time of writing.
☎ 04 66 65 60 01 for information.

Coopérative des Artisans de Lozère

4 Rue de l'Ange
Mende
Open: All year, Monday-Saturday
9am-12noon, 2-7pm (but closed
on Monday September to June) .
☎ 04 66 65 01 57.

Château de Castanet

Nr Villefort
Open: mid-June to mid-September,
daily 10am-12noon, 2-6pm.
☎ 04 66 46 81 11.

Wolves of Gévaudan

CÉVENNES NATIONAL PARK

From Le Bleymard the Cévennes National Park in Lozère is explored by the D20 that crosses the Col de Finiels. On this road the Chalet du Mont Lozère is famous with pony-trekkers, walkers and cross-country skiers. From it a footpath leads to the Sommet de Finiels (assigned, oval route: allow 3 hours). The summit, at 5,573ft (1,699m), is an excellent viewpoint. Beyond the Col de Finiels the road descends to Le Pont-de-Montvert. The asymmetric, but nonetheless delightful, bridge over the infant Tarn in the village has a curious tower at one end. This is an old toll-house, folk crossing the river here in medieval times having to pay for the privilege.

Florac

The Toll House & the Camisards

After Louis XIV, the Sun King, had revoked the Edict of Nantes, in 1685, there was a long period of passive resistance from the Protestants of central France to the King's attempt to create a unified, Catholic state. As part of the King's policy the Abbé Langlade du Chayla was appointed as Inspector of Missions (that is, seeker of Protestants) in the Cévennes. The Abbé took his work seriously, taking over the toll-house and imprisoning and torturing Camisards in its lower rooms. Finally, local patience was exhausted and on the evening of 24 July 1702 Esprit Séguier, a wool trade worker, led a group of men across the bridge intent on freeing the prisoners. Du Chayla's men fired on the Camisards but the group succeeded in breaking into the house. The prisoners were released, Du Chayla's men escaped by jumping from the windows, but du Chayla himself broke a leg in the jump. He was set upon and stabbed to death. The Camisard war had begun.

North-west of Montvert – take the D35, another narrow, tortuous road – is **Runes**, a delightful granite-built village. From it a 20 minute walk southwards reaches a point where the water of the Mirals streams leaps 190ft (58m) in a series of four falls into a wide, shallow pool. Northwards there is a small chaos, a region of huge boulders created by erosion and scattered by glacial action.

The main route through the Cévennes is the N106 which heads south through forested country to reach the **Col de Montmirat**. To the east from the Col the D35 leads up towards the Cévennes.

Turn left to find **La Fage** one of the best villages in which to see the complete range of traditional architecture. Here there is a bread oven, once shared by the entire village, the forge, where cattle would be branded and oxen shod before being driven to market, the fountain, the cross, which was always set up in hamlets remote from the parish church, and a bell tower. The bell was rung on dark or stormy nights when it was known that villagers were returning from market. The towers were known as Tempest Belfries, a name deriving from a part of the consecration service, the bell being set up to 'call the living, pity the dead and repel storms'.

South of the Col de Montmirat is **Florac**, a charming town set in the valley of the Tarnon, a tributary of the Tarn, and protected by the cliffs of the **Rocher de Rochefort**. In the past the town's strategic position, at the edge of the **Causse Méjean** and at the mouth of the valley between the Montagne du Bouges and the southern Cévennes peaks, made it much fought over. Its castle was destroyed and rebuilt several times, then served as a prison during the Wars of Religion.

Today it is the headquarters of the Cévennes National Park and has a fine Information Centre. The town is worth exploring: there is a sixteenth-century house that was once occupied by the Knights Templar, a nineteenth-century Huguenot chapel and a Catholic church from the same period. During the religious conflict in the town the Prot-

• IN THE STEPS OF ROBERT LOUIS STEVENSON •

Those who follow the D998 east of Florac follow in the footsteps of Robert Louis Stevenson whose book, on his donkey-assisted walk – *Travels with a Donkey in the Cévennes* – has become a classic. Stevenson set out at 9am on Sunday 22 September 1878 from Le Monastier-sur-Gazelle, a village a short distance from Le Puy-en-Velay. Stevenson did not like Le Monastier, claiming it was noteworthy for drunkenness, its inhabitants having 'laid aside even the civility of speech'.

He must have been glad to leave, though the pleasure was short-lived, his chosen companion, a donkey called Modestine, being a disaster. Stevenson was camping, unusual for the time, and needed a pack-animal. A horse would have been ideal, a donkey that was on heat and could travel only at a 'snail's gallop' was not. Not only did Stevenson have difficulty persuading the donkey to move, but he could not get the hang of the pack saddle either, his pack continually falling off. To cap it all, the weather was dreadful.

Things did improve eventually. Stevenson and Modestine crossed the Cévennes then followed the Tarn to Florac. He then continued to St Jean-du-Gard where he parted company with Modestine, claiming that he shed a tear as he did so. Presumably a tear of joy.

estants demolished the Catholic church and used the stone to build their own church, only to see the process reversed a few years later.

Place Dides (near the castle) and the view of the Pêcher from the nearby bridge make a journey to the town worthwhile on their own. A longer walk visits the Source du Pêcher – follow the signed Sentier du Castor beside the castle: the walk has illustrated boards with information on various aspects of the town and walk.

Southward from Florac, take the D983, leftwards from the D907, to reach the **Corniche des Cévennes**. But before following that superb road, turn left to visit **Barre-des-Cévennes**. In medieval times a castle stood on the Castellas, the hill above the village. There was a signal tower, too, part of a system that passed messages across the Cévennes. From

Barre the D62 leads to **Plan de Fontmort** and **Mont Mars**.

Mont Mars

The peak's name is thought to derive from the god Mercury – whose name the Gauls often shortened to Merc. A local story tells of an old woman who, despite her age and being single, gave birth near the peak and was condemned to roam the area carrying a huge rock as a penance. Sadly her baby died at Plan de Fontmort (the name being from d'Enfant Mort) and her donkey drowned in a river at Négase (from *noie ane* – drowned ass). Still having to carry the rock the old woman started to climb Mont Mars, but collapsed and died at Pierre de la Vieille (the stone of the old woman).

Continued on page 92...

The Park was set up not only to protect the magnificent scenery and unique ecology of this area of France, but to preserve the way of life of the inhabitants. Over 1,200 species of flowers have been identified within the Park, of which 20 are unique to the Cévennes. There are 40 species of orchids and in spring the daffodils are beautiful, but most impressive of all the flowers, is the Martagon Lily, a beautiful plant with pink-spotted, purple flowers that curl back to reveal deep pink stamens.

Some 45 types of mammal, over 20 reptiles and 150 species of bird have been noted, together with countless types of butterflies and other insects. Of the animals, the rare genet, the wild boar (*sanglier*) and the beaver would be the most popular sightings.

The birds include the capercaille (re-introduced after becoming extinct in the eighteenth century), red-legged partridge, black woodpecker, snow finch, stone curlew, wall creeper, golden eagle, Scops owl and eagle owl. During the migration season short-toed eagles and honey buzzards are also seen.

The most distinctive tree of the Cévennes is the sweet chestnut. It is believed that the tree was introduced to the area in the

eleventh century, after which it spread rapidly, mostly as a result of human activity. In an area of relatively poor soil where cereals did not grow well, the chestnut soon became the staple diet of the local folk. Chestnuts were ground to produce a flour – chestnut flour based bread and cakes can still be bought. They were eaten fresh – *cousinat*, a fresh chestnut-based stew is still a local specialty – and dried for winter eating. The small stone drying houses, called *clèdes*, can still be seen. The nuts were also fed to goats and pigs, while sheep fed on fresh chestnut shoots. Longer shoots were woven into baskets and chestnut wood was used to make furniture and fencing. Even the bark was utilized, being a good source of tannin.

The Cévennes is a superb area for walking, a whole map of GRs crossing the upland areas, as well as exploring the valleys. The country is ideally suited for exploration, being criss-crossed with tracks, many of which are *drailles*. This very old Provençal word defines a sheep track, usually one used during the transhumances.

The stone stands about 40 minutes' walk from the road – take the road from Barre to St Germain-de-Calberte and from there go south on the D984 towards St Jean-du-Gard: stop at Pont de Burgen and follow GR67A eastwards. The stone stands where GR67 splits into two arms (67A and 67B), on the flank of the Montagne de la Vieille Mort, the mountain of the old dead woman.

The Corniche des Cévennes follows an old route through the Cévennes: an official note from the early eighteenth century states that the route is inadequate for modern transport – ie carriages. The problem was that the armies of Louis XIV could not easily move into the area in their quest for Camisards. By royal decree, therefore, a better road was constructed. That road is a joy for the visitor.

It passes **St Laurent-de-Trèves**, above which significant dinosaur fossil remains have been discovered. It travels through **L'Hospitalet**, close to where the Camisards held secret meetings, crosses the **Col de Solperière** and descends to **Le Pompidou**, a village set among chestnut groves. Beyond, the road travels along the border between Lozère and Gard, with the peaks of

Places to Visit

Cévennes National Park (Lozère)

Ecomuseums on Mont Lozère

The **Maison du Mont Lozère** in Le Pont-de-Montvert has collections on the natural history and way of life of Mont Lozère and the folk who live on its flanks.

Maison du Mont Lozère

Le Pont-de-Montvert
Open: mid-April to September, daily 10.30am-12.30pm, 2.30-6.30pm.
☎ 04 66 45 80 73.

The **Mas Camargue** to the north-east of Montvert is a particular form of farmhouse built with massive walls. A signed walk takes visitors past a mill, sheepfolds etc to illustrate the various aspects of Cévennes farming.

Mas Camargue

Nr Le Pont-de-Montvert
Open: Any reasonable time.
☎ 04 66 45 80 73.

The **Ferme de Troubat**, east of Montvert, is a restored red granite farm with mill and bread oven.

Ferme de Troubat

Nr Le Pont-de-Montvert
Open: mid-June to mid-September, daily except Thursday and Friday 10.30am-12.30pm, 2.30-6.30pm (open daily in July and August).
☎ 04 66 45 80 73.

The **Mas de la Barque** is reached by heading south from Villefort. Here, a signed walk from the old house illustrates the life of a Mont Lozère forester.

Mas de la Barque

Nr Villefort
Open: Any reasonable time.
☎ 04 66 45 80 73.

the Cévennes picked out on either side. In the morning or evening, when the light is angled and the heat haze has decreased, this is a memorable journey.

CAUSSE DE SAUVETERRE

To the west of Mende and Florac lies the Causse de Sauveterre, the least arid and most intensively farmed of the four Grands Causses. The road across it – from La Canourgue to Ste-Énimie in the Gorges du Tarn – passes the Sabot de Malepyre, a large clog-shaped rock pierced by a natural arch – to reach the D32. A short distance to the west is Le Villard, a fascinating village. Because of its position, the village was heavily fortified in medieval times and sections of the castle and ramparts still exist.

To the west of the igneous blocks of **Mont Lozère** and the high Cévennes lie the *causses*, high limestone plateaux bisected by deep river valleys. The limestone sheet of the plateaux was laid down uniformly, but in time the Tarn, Jonte and Dourbie rivers divided it into four blocks. The Causses of Sauveterre and Méjean lie in the *département* of Lozère, while those of Noir and Larzac lie to the south.

The limestone of the *causses* is carboniferous, a rock which is permeable to water. The immediate effect of this is that the soil is thin and dry, the vegetation sparse and poor. Add to this a harsh climate of hot, dry summers and cold winters during which the area is subject to piercing winds and an arid, almost desolate country is created. Yet the effects of erosion by wind and water have also been to create a land of geographical delights, caves, gorges, and cirques, to entrance the visitors. The **Gorges du Tarn** are one of the great natural wonders of France. Though not as spectacularly vast as the Verdon Gorge in Provence, or even as the Ardèche Gorge, the Tarn gorges have the advantage of a road that runs beside the river, so that the cliff scenery can be viewed at first hand, as it were. The disadvantage is that in summer months the road can be one long traffic jam, especially at weekends. The best trip, therefore, is early morning or late afternoon – though as much of the gorge runs north-south that does mean losing some of the light which plays on the cliffs and water – or to visit out of season: in September the gorge is usually quiet whilst shades and tints are wonderful. The alternative – taking to the water and enjoying the cliff scenery at even closer quarters – is almost as good.

Tarn Gorge from Roc de Hourtous (looking west)

Eventually water flowing down through the limestone of the causses reaches an impervious rock layer, usually marl. The stream now flows along that layer. In time major rivers are created and the cave roofs above them collapse or are dissolved away forming gorges. The effect of this is most clearly seen in the Gorges du Tarn. The gorge is consistently tight, sometimes only 100ft (30m) wide and the sides steep. But most interesting of all is the fact that no tributary streams flow into the Tarn as it traverses the gorge. All entry water is from resurgences, points where underground water resurfaces. Over forty resurgences enter the Tarn, some of them as delightful waterfalls. Our trip down the Tarn starts from Florac heading north then turning left to **Ispagnac**, a village sometimes called the Garden of Lozère for the fertility of the land beside the Tarn. Beyond is **Quezac**, which has a quaint Gothic bridge and a church built on the spot where, in 1050, a statue of the Virgin was uncovered. There is no satisfactory explanation for the discovery, which was viewed at the time as miraculous. Even the Pope, Urbain V, journeyed here to see it.

Above the village are the ruins of the **Château de Rocheblave**, built in the sixteenth century to protect the entrance to the gorge. Rocheblave sits above the river's right bank, the left bank being protected by the **Château de Charbonnières**, a little further downstream. Further on, but on the same side is **Castelbouc**, where the ruins of another castle overhang a small village.

The next castle, **Château de Prades** is in a better state of health, and can be visited. It was built in

Right: Tarn Gorge, near le Rozier

Below: Canoeists neering a waterfall, Tarn Gorge

Castelbouc

The story is told of the knight who occupied the castle during the twelfth century. He lived a life of pleasure and excess while most of his contemporaries were away risking their lives in Crusades. Eventually the man died – during another heavy bout of drinking and eating – but his soul was compelled to roam the cliffs above the Tarn as a giant goat. This goat so terrified the castle's next owners that they abandoned the building. The goat took possession, and the site has been the *castel bouc*, the castle of the goat, ever since. In the sixteenth century the castle was occupied by bandits who terrorized the local area until soldiers evicted them, partially destroying the castle to prevent re-occupation.

the thirteenth century, an early attempt to hold the mouth of the gorge, though its major action was three centuries later when its Catholic defenders held out against a prolonged onslaught by a Protestant army.

The castle, with its excellent views of the river, is very atmospheric. Beyond it, is **Ste-Énimie**, the best of Tarn villages. Ste-Énimie was a seventh-century Merovingian princess, daughter of Clotaire and brother of Dagobert, who wished to become a nun but whose father wanted her to marry a suitable prince. A suitor was found, but Énimie contracted leprosy when he was brought to court. Hardly surprisingly he quickly went home.

An angel then visited the girl, telling her to travel to a spring here in the gorge where her leprosy would be cured. It was cured, but returned when she went home to her father's palace. Seeing this as a sign from God, Énimie returned to Tarn, living out her life as a solitary hermit, sustained by food brought by pilgrims and water from a spring. The spring, the **Fontaine de Burle**, can still be

seen – go north from the Post Office.

Elsewhere, any walk through the village will be worthwhile. The remains of an old monastery, gutted by fire at the time of the Revolution, lie to the north. Beside the fine church – inside which Ste-Énimie's legend is told on a series of modern ceramic tiles – is **Le Vieux Logis**, an ecomuseum with exhibits on the lifestyle of the inhabitants of the area during the last century. Close to the museum is the Place du Beurre and the old market hall, the focal point of the old village.

St Chély-du-Tarn, the next village downstream, is less well-known than Ste-Énimie, but with its waterfall resurgence, is no less delightful. The bridge over the Tarn is believed to be Roman, and the fine Romanesque church has a delightful external stairway. Above the village there is a twelfth-century chapel built into the rock, beyond which the walking visitor can reach the **Cirque de St Chély**, less picturesque than Navacelles, but interesting nonetheless. Close by, but across the river, there is another cirque – **Cirque de Pougnadoires**, above the village of the same name.

Moving on downstream, the visitor passes the **Château de la Caze**, a beautiful castle, built in the fifteenth century and now restored as a hotel/restaurant. Next is **La Malène**. Here a route linking the *causses* of Sauveterre and Méjean crosses the Tarn: a transhumance of sheep and cattle fording the river here must have been a wonderful sight. At the village the visitor can board a boat to explore the tightest part of the gorge, **Les Détroits** (The Narrows), and the **Cirque des Baumes**.

The village can also be used to explore two superb viewpoints of the gorge: head south along D16, going steeply up on to the Causse Méjean, bear right at La Croix-Blanche, then turn right past the village of Rieisse and follow signs to **Roc des Hourtous** and **Roc du Serre**. The first named is reached by car, but a 15 minute walk is needed to reach the second. From either of these viewpoints (but especially the first) the view of the gorge is incomparable.

Beyond The Narrows and the Cirque des Baumes the Tarn turns sharp left and flows past the **Pas de Souci**.

From **Les Vignes**, the next village, a road leads up to **Pointe Sublime**, by common consent the finest viewpoint of the Gorge. The viewpoint is set above the Cirque des Baumes and takes in a long, beautiful section of the narrowest part of the gorge. Beyond Les Vignes the gorge narrows again, offering splendid views all the way to **Le Rozier** where the Tarn joins the Jonte.

Le Rozier has an enviable position, but **Peyreleau**, set just across the Jonte is the prettier village. From either there are possibilities of exploration. Southwards, but over the border from Languedoc, is **Montpellier-le-Vieux**, the best example of a r*oches ruiniformes*. This superb chaos was held in awe by locals who thought it was the remnants of a village destroyed for its ungodliness and would not go near it. Only in the nineteenth century was it finally explored.

Ste-Énimie and the Devil

Legend has it that at the Pas de Souci Ste-Énimie caught sight of the Devil while out walking. Seeing her, the Devil fled, so Ste-Énimie fell to her knees and prayed: in response rocks fell from the high cliffs, cutting off the Devil's escape, though they were only partially successful, the Devil escaping back to Hell through a nearby cave. The name is from *soussitch*, a landslide, though it is more likely that this was caused by an earthquake in 580AD rather than a diabolical jogger.

Roches Ruiniformes

Although the limestone of the Causses is calcium-based there are occasional nodules of a magnesium-rich rock called dolomite, a rock better known for the spires and towers created from it in north-eastern Italy (though the name derives from Dolomieu, a French geologist). Dolomite is more resistant to weathering than the softer calcium-based rock and in an outcrop of mixed rock tends to remain after the softer rock has weathered away. The result is a weird assembly of rocks of fantastic shapes which, when viewed from a distance, can look like the towers and houses of a town: the name means 'town-ruin rocks'. The best example of this type of formation is Montpellier-le-Vieux (old Montpellier) in the *département* of Aveyron.

CAUSSE MÉJEAN

The Gorges de la Jonte that head eastward from Le Rozier are less dramatic that those of the Tarn, but no less delightful, the wooded slopes and white cliffs being wonderfully picturesque. The first place of note is Meyrueis, a village set close to where two streams join the Jonte. The village is an excellent base for exploration and, at an altitude of 2,300ft (700m), offers a little coolness to counteract summer's heat.

Causse Méjean, above Florac

Above & right: Aven Armand

Below: Water draining down through the limestone of the causses means that domestic animals find little to drink. The farmers therefore create lavognes, shallow depressions lined with clay, to hold water. This one is on Causse Méjean.

To the north the D986 can be followed up on to **Causse Méjean**, the road offering perhaps the best view along the Jonte Gorge. On the Causse is **Aven Armand,** arguably Europe's finest show cave and even, perhaps, the best in the world. The cave started, as all av*ens*, with water percolating down through the Causse Méjean. The chimneys this created eventually joined to form a chamber into which collapsed the remnants of many of the chimneys.

On top of this huge pile of rubble stalagmites have grown, creating the Fôret Vierge, the Virgin's Forest. Many of the names given to show cave formations are, at best, ludicrous, but here the word forest is apt. There are around 400 stalagmites, some 10ft (3m) in diameter, many 50-65ft (15-20m) high. One 100ft (30m) specimen is probably the tallest known stalagmite in the world. The chamber holding the forest is vast – 200ft by 350ft and 140ft tall (60m by 110m and up to 50m high) – and is exquisitely lit. The cave was first entered by Louis Armand, a partner of Édouard Martel, the greatest of French speliologists. After Armand's descent, Martel entered the cave. Of his return to the outside he said 'I came out as if from a dream'. It is easy to see why.

Beyond the cave the D986 traverses the Causse – offering another route to the viewpoints of Hourtous and Serre. This is one of the very best Causse drives, the flat, arid plateau being seen to perfection. Here and there are little villages, adding to the charm.

Close to Meyrueis there is another cave. The **Grotte de Dargilan** was discovered in 1880 when a shepherd chased a fox into a crack in the rock. Later, Édouard Martel explored the cave, discovering a considerable length of passage beyond the vast Grande Salle du Chaos. Six chambers of the 20 so far discovered in this huge system are open to the public, but visitors going beyond the Grande Salle need to be reasonably fit – there are more than 300 steps to be negotiated.

The Grotte is reached along the D39. On the other route out of Meyrueis, the D986, stands the **Château de Roquedols a** large fifteenth/sixteenth-century quadrilateral castle with two round towers. The castle has a fine Renaissance staircase, some old furniture and houses an information office for the Cévennes National Park.

Finally from Meyrueis, the edge of the Causse Méjean can be followed back to Florac. On this road, a left turn at the Col de Perjuret leads to the **Chaos de Nîmes-le-Vieux.** Park at the hamlets of L'Hem or Veygalier and walk to the site – just a few minutes are needed. Although not as good as Montpellier-le-Vieux the site is an interesting one, worth visiting if you are unable to find time to visit the more famous chaos, or want a quieter visit. At **Veygalier t**here is a small geological exhibition exploring the creation of the Causses and some of their features. The exhibition includes a fascinating trail.

Southern Lozère

Florac Château (Cévennes National Park Information Centre)

Open: June to mid-September, daily 9am-7pm; mid-September to May, daily 8am-12noon, 2-6pm (Monday to Friday only mid-November to Easter).

☎ 04 66 49 53 01.

Château de Prades

Gorges du Tarn
Open: July and August, daily except Sunday 10am-12.30pm, 2.30-6.30pm. Open at other times of the year on a variable basis.

☎ 04 42 26 60 75.

Le Vieux Logis

Ste-Énimie
Open: July and August, daily 10am-12.30pm, 2-7pm. April to June, September, daily 10am-12noon, 2.30-6pm.

☎ 04 66 48 53 44.

Chaos de Montpellier-le-Vieux

Nr Le Rozier
Open: mid-March to October, daily 9am-7pm. November to mid-March, by request.

☎ 05 65 60 66 30.

Aven Armand

Nr Meyrueis
Open: June to August, daily 9.30am-7pm; mid-March to May, daily 9.30am-12noon, 1.30-6pm; September to mid-November, 9.30am-12noon, 1.30-5pm.

☎ 04 66 45 61 31.

A combined ticket is available for the cave and Montpellier-le-Vieux

Grotte de Dargilan

Nr Meyrueis
Open: July and August, daily 9am-7pm; April to June and September, daily 9am-12noon, 1.30-6pm; October, daily 10am-12noon, 1.30-5pm.

☎ 04 65 45 60 20.

Château de Roquedols

Nr Meyrueis
Open: July and August, daily except Monday mornings and Sunday afternoons 9.30am-12.30pm, 3-6.30pm.

☎ 04 66 45 60 33.

Chaos de Nîmes-le-Vieux

Nr Meyrueis
Open at any reasonable time
☎ 04 66 45 60 33 for information.

Exposition Géologique

Veygalier
Open: Easter to September, daily 9am-8pm.

☎ 04 66 45 65 45.

Aude

4

The geography of Aude could be said to mirror that of Hérault, with beautiful hills giving way to a plain dotted with picturesque villages and, finally, a coastline of fine beaches. But though the hills of the Montagne Noire are certainly beautiful and the gorges of the southern *département* spectacular, Aude's uplands do not have the wild majesty of the Causses. The loss, though, is compensated for by a series of old fortresses that are as romantic and interesting as their sites are improbable. Aude is Cathar country, one of the most historically interesting and, in some ways, historically important landscape in France. And at the heart of it is Carcassonne, arguably the finest medieval town in Europe.

CASTELNAUDARY AND CARCASSONNE

Visitors to Languedoc who choose to arrive by plane in Toulouse and to hire a car , usually make their way immediately to the autoroute and turn eastwards, anxious to reach Carcassonne. Such haste is understandable, but it inevitably means that the westernmost part of Aude is missed. Those who have the time should take the N113, a fast road with arrow-straight sections between its gentle curves. Aude is soon reached and the road, keeping to the crest of a ridge of land, offers long views over wheatfields and vineyards, with fields of sunflowers adding splashes of yellow to the many shades of green and the occasional avenue of plane trees that are such a feature of older French roads. This country is the Lauragais, an important farming area for centuries.

Castelnaudary, a town just off the N113, is now the area's largest town, but in medieval times the capital was **St Papoul**, a village to the east, along the D103. The abbey here was founded in 768 by Pepin the Short, the first Carolingian king and father of Charlemagne. Later, in the fourteenth century, concerned over another upsurge of heretical beliefs, the Pope made the abbot a bishop, forcing him to forsake spiritual isolation for keeping a close eye on the locals. The abbey, with its fine cloisters, is open to visitors, as is the equally fine fourteenth-century Romanesque cathedral. Eventually St Papoul became a quiet backwater: today its old medieval houses are a delight for the visitor.

Castelnaudary, which seems occasionally to became lost in all the talk of cassoulet, is quiet and pretty, the Cours de la République being a fine, tree-shaded boulevard. To the north, the **Moulin du Cugarel**, is a restored seventeenth-century windmill, one of many that once stood on the Lauragais plain.

At Castelnaudary the Canal du Midi enters the Grand Bassin, a broad lake where barges and boats could (and still can) be turned. Heading eastwards out of the basin is a series of locks which drop vessels back down to the narrow, tree-shaded canal. The town is a well-liked spot for visitors exploring the canal and there are several places where boats can be hired. To the north of the basin, in a sixteenth-century mansion that once housed the local tribunal and is still known as the **Présidial**, is a small museum that explores the ancient history of Lauragais.

Carcassonne lies at an elbow of the River Aude. The river rises in the Pyrenees, but flows northwards at first before turning sharply right to flow towards the Mediterranean.

Continued on page 108...

Cassoulet

Castelnaudary is the undisputed birthplace of cassoulet, a fact of which the town and, it would seem, every one of its restaurants is proud. The perfect cassoulet, that most distinctive of Languedocian dishes – needs – according to just about every French cook book ever written – four main ingredients: Lavelanet white beans, Castelnaudary water, a casserole dish made of clay from Issel and a fire made of wood cut on the Montagne Noire.

Cassoulet has a long history. Once the staple of peasants it rose to being the dish of the aristocracy – though this seems, in part, to have been due to a widely held belief that it cured sterility and was, therefore, an aphrodisiac. Today it is both staple and delicacy, available in tins in supermarkets and as ready-to-heat-and-serve take-aways in charcuteries. It is also the subject of serious talk among gourmets and the chefs of the Grande Confrérie du Cassoulet de Castelnaudary, a brotherhood that keeps alive (or creates) the mystique of the dish.

On the site of La Cité, as Carcassonne's medieval city is now called, there was a defended settlement as early as the sixth century BC. Later the Gauls occupied the site, calling it Carcasso. When the Romans occupied Languedoc they further fortified it, calling it Julia Carcasso. When the Romans left, the Visigoths held the site for 300 years until it was conquered by the Saracens on their push through Spain. The Franks forced the Saracens back, retaking the city but leaving it on the border between the Frankish kingdom and Catalonia. There it stayed until 1659 when that part of the Catalonian region of Roussillon lying to the north of the Pyrenees was incorporated into France.

In the wake of the Frankish successes, Carcassonne was ruled by the Viscounts Trencavel who also held Albi, Nîmes and Béziers. Though in the domain of the Counts of Toulouse, the Trencavels were powerful princes in their own right, and at Carcassonne they built a strong castle, the Château Comtal.

It was to this castle that Raymond-Roger Trencavel retreated when the army of the Albigensian Crusade headed inland from Béziers after the massacre of its inhabitants in July 1209. The army arrived on 1 August. It was a blisteringly hot summer and the inhabitants of Carcassonne were soon succumbing to a mixture of flies and poor sanitation. When offered safe passage, provided they left 'bearing only their sins', the besieged folk, some of whom had escaped Béziers, must have wondered whether the Crusaders could be trusted. But with no alternative they accepted. Astonishingly, Simon de Montfort and Bishop Arnaud Amaury were as good as their word. Raymond-Roger Trencavel was taken prisoner and died soon after, poisoned, or so it is said, by de Montfort, who took both his title and his estates.

Having secured Languedoc the French king improved the fortifications of his frontier city, building a defensive wall and, later, adding an inner wall, each defended by a series of towers.

After Roussillon had become part of France the fortress was no longer needed and fell into disrepair. It was used as a quarry by the locals and what remained of the walls and towers were excavated by poor folk who lived within the structure. It is likely that today little or nothing would remain, but in 1844 Eugène Viollet-le-Duc started massive restoration. Viollet-le-Duc was a romantic living in a romantic age and his restoration has been criticized for its inaccuracies – particularly the pepper-pot tower roofs – but overall it is agreed that La Cité today is a fair reflection of the thirteenth-century city. It is not exact – but without squalid conditions, dirt, poor sanitation and over-crowding it can never be, and if they were restored who would bother to come.

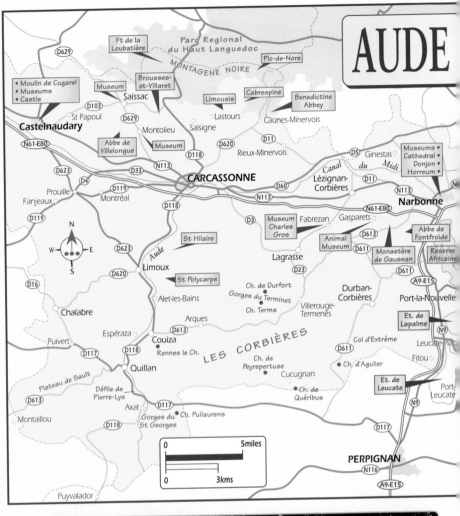

AUDE

- Moulin de Cugarel
- Museums
- Castle

Ft de la Loubatière

Parc Regional du Haut Languedoc

MONTAGENE NOIRE

Pic-de-Nore

Brousses-et-Villaret

Museum

Saissac

Cabrespine

Limousis

Benedictine Abbey

St Papoul

Castelnaudary

D629

D103

Montolieu

Lastours

Salsigne

Caunes-Minervois

Abbe de Villelongue

Museum

Rieux-Minervois

D11

D620

Ginestas

Museums •
Cathedral •
Donjon •
Horreum •

D5

Canal

du

Midi

Lézignan-Corbières

N113

D118

CARCASSONNE

D60

D11

Prouille

Fanjeaux

Montréal

N113

Narbonne

N61-E80

Gasparets

Museum Charles Gros

Fabrezan

Abbe de Fontfroide

D3

Animal Museum

D613

Reserve Africaine

St Hilaire

Aude

Monastère de Gaussan

D611

Limoux

Lagrasse

D23

D611

St Polycarpe

Ch. de Durfort

Gorges du Terminet

Durban-Corbières

Port-la-Nouvelle

Alet-les-Bains

Ch. Terms

Villerouge-Termenès

Et. de Lapalme

A9-E15

Arques

Chalabre

Espéraza

D613

Couiza

Rennes le Ch.

LES CORBIÈRES

Col d'Extréme

Leucate-Plag

Puivert

D117

D118

Quillan

Ch. de Peyrepertuse

Cucugnan

Ch. d'Aguilier

Fitou

D611

Plateau de Sault

Défile de Pierre-Lys

Ch. de Quéribus

Et. de Leucate

Port-Leucate

Montaillou

Axat

Gorges du St Georges

Cb. Puilaurens

D117

D117

N9

| 0 | | 5miles |
| 0 | | 3kms |

PERPIGNAN

N116

A9-E15

Puyvalador

Grand Bassin, Castelnaudary

Above: Carcassonne

Right: Puppetter, Carcassonne

Below: Château Comtal, Carcassonne

The fact that a relatively straightforward route to Toulouse and northern France existed by turning left where the Aude turned right made the river's elbow a site of great strategic importance: here a corridor from the Mediterranean to Toulouse met a corridor over the Pyrenees into Catalonia.

From a distance Carcassonne La Cité is the walled, be-towered city of fairy tales, especially if viewed on misty mornings. Most visitors enter through Porte Narbonnaise – though there are actually several gateways into the city. The pits to either side of the fortified bridge here were never water filled, having been dug simply to impede the progress of siege engines. Ahead now is Rue Cros-Mayrevieille, lined with souvenir shops, cafés and restaurants, but with occasional shops that remind the visitor that people still live here. The road leads to the Place du Château where modern street performers re-invent the troubadours' art.

Here a gateway leads into the Château Comtal's barbican. Beyond is the castle that now houses the **Musée Lapidaire**, a fine collection of statuary and stonework dating from the fourth to sixteenth centuries. Included in the collection are a group of medieval headstones. These circular stones have a cross on one side and a carving representing the dead man's profession, an axe, a hammer etc, on the back.

At the Barbican gateway the visitor can turn left through another crowded street to reach the more peaceful square beside the Basilica of St Nazaire. The Basilica is a fine building – started in the eleventh century, and finished in magnificent Gothic style in the thirteenth – with beautiful stained glass and some excellent works of art. Close to it there is a stone stairway up on to a section of the inner wall ramparts, from where there is a fine view of the basilica and a glimpse of the modern outdoor theatre that lies between it and the inner wall.

From the bottom of the stairway a right turn into Rue du Plô leads to Place Marcou and back to Porte Narbonnaise. Just a few steps away are Les Lices, the lists, named for the jousting practice and tournaments that used to take place there. They circle the city, offering a close-up view of the architecture of medieval warfare.

In the excitement of a visit to La Cité it is easy to forget that at the base of its hill there is another city, Carcassonne Ville Basse. This lower city was built in the late Middle Ages, its streets laid out on a square grid, and is reached over the fourteenth-century Pont Vieux or the much less elegant Pont Neuf. The eighteenth-century Fontaine de Neptune in Place Carnot is worth visiting and the **Musée des Beaux-Arts**, in the eighteenth century Présidial, while not quite living up to its name, is worthwhile for those interested in European painting of the seventeenth and eighteenth centuries.

MONTAGNE NOIRE

North of Carcassonne lies the main mass of the **Montagne Noire** whose eastern flank runs into the Hérault. This Black Mountain, so called because of its dark tree covering, forms the bulk of the **Haut Languedoc Regional Park**. In ancient times the hills were mined for copper and iron, and although this has ceased the mining tradition lives on at a gold mine near **Salsigne**. Large stands of chestnuts on the hill flanks and in the valleys again speak of the tree's importance to the subsistence farmers of medieval times. The native trees also produced building timber and charcoal: today the logging tradition lives on, but with plantations of foreign pines and firs replacing the slower growing native trees.

Montagne Noire is still in its tourist infancy, its tight valleys and narrow roads discouraging many visitors despite those valleys being the very feature that make a visit worthwhile. **Montolieu**, a small town, has been a focus for paper making for many years and has a small museum to printing and the graphic arts as well as a number of bookshops. The paper mill at nearby **Brousses-et-Villaret** can be visited.

Turn left at Montolieu to reach the **Abbaye de Villelongue**, a well-preserved monastery dating from the late twelfth century. **Saissac** has a small museum with an interesting collection of tools from the old Montagne Noire trades. The village itself is wonderfully picturesque, built close to a gorge and surrounded by wooded hills.

North-east of Saissac the **Prise d'Eau d'Alzeau** is the main 'top-up' lake for the Canal du Midi. Nearby is a monument to Pierre-Paul Riquet. North-east again is the **Forêt de la Loubatière**, a large area of original oak wood. East of the forest **Mas-Cabardès** is a pretty village of half-timbered houses around a sixteenth-century church with an octagonal tower. The cross at the middle of the village is also sixteenth century, the gift of the Weavers Guild, grateful for the village's contribution of pure water and water power to their trade.

Southwards now are the **Châteaux de Lastours**. There are no less than four castles on the hill top here, two that preceded the Albigensian Crusade (one resisted a siege by Simon de Montfort, but was later surrendered to him) and two more constructed by the French king to hold his new lands.

The Saut de Roland

Near the Lastours castles the Saut de Roland is a horse's hoofprint-like mark on a boulder. Legend has it that the famous French knight was pursuing a dragon over the Montagne Noire and his horse left its hoof print in the rock.

To the west of Lastours is Salsigne, with its gold mine, while to the east, at **Limousis** there is a fine show cave. In it pools of still water reflect the beautiful formations. One of the formations is over 30ft (9m) across and is known as Le Lustre (chandelier). In the next valley to the east, near **Cabrespine** there is another show cave, a more spectacular one with beautifully tinted formations, though there is nothing which quite matches Le Lustre. North of Cabrespine is the **Pic de Noire**, at 1,210m (3,969ft) perhaps the finest of all viewpoints in the range.

Northern Aude

St Papoul Abbey

Nr Castelnaudary
Open: July and August,
daily 10am-7pm ; May, June, September and October, daily 10am-12noon,
2-6pm (5pm in October) .
☎: 04 68 94 97 75.

Moulin de Cugarel

Castelnaudary
Open: mid-June to mid-September,
Monday-Saturday 10am-12noon,
3-6.30pm, Sunday 3-6pm.
☎: 04 68 23 05 73.

Musée Archéologique du Présidial

Castelnaudary
Open: July and August, Tuesday-Saturday 10am-12noon, 3-7pm,
Monday and Sunday 3-7pm.
☎: 04 68 23 05 73 or 04 68 23 00 42.

Château Comtal/Musée Lapidaire

Carcassonne La Cité
Open: June to September,
daily 9am-7pm (7.30pm in July and August); October to May, daily
9.30am-12.30pm, 2-5pm
(6pm in May and October).
☎: 04 68 25 01 66.

Musée des Beaux-Arts

1 Rue de Verdun,
Carcassonne Ville Basse
Open: mid-June to mid-September,
Wednesday to Sunday 10am-12noon,
2-6pm; mid-September to mid-June,
Tuesday to Saturday 10am-12noon,
2-6pm.
☎: 04 68 77 73 70.

Museum of Printing and Graphic Arts

Montolieu
Open: April to October, daily 2-6pm
(7.30pm June to September); November to March, daily 9.30am-5pm.
☎: 04 68 24 80 04 or 04 68 24 80 71.

Paper Mill

Brousses-et-Villaret
Open: July to mid-September, guided tours daily 11am-6pm; mid-September to June guided tours, Monday-Friday at 11am and 4pm, Saturday and Sunday, 11am-5.30pm.
☎: 04 68 26 67 43.

Abbaye de Villelonge

Nr Montolieu
Open: May to October,
daily 10am-12noon, 2-6.30pm.
☎: 04 68 76 00 81.

Town Museum (Musée des Vieux Metiers)

Saissac
Open: mid-June to mid-September,
daily 10am-12.30pm, 2.30-6.30pm;
mid-September to December and
mid-April to mid-June, Sunday
10.30am-12noon, 3-6.30pm;
January to mid-April, Sundays 3-6pm.
☎: 04 68 24 47 80.

Châteaux de Lastours

Open: July and August, daily 9am-8pm; April to June and September,
daily 10am-6pm; October to March,
Saturday and Sunday 10am-5pm.
☎: 04 68 77 56 02.

Grotte de Limousis

Open: July and August, daily 10am-6pm; March to June and September,
daily 10am-12noon, 2-5.30pm.
☎: 04 68 77 50 26.

Gouffre de Cabrespine

Open: July and August, daily 10am-7pm; March to June and September to November, daily 10am-12noon,
2-6pm.
☎: 04 68 26 14 22.

BLACK MOUNTAINS TO NARBONNE

To the south of the Black Mountains is Caunes-Minervois, a small town whose name notes the change from the high Black Mountain to the lower hills of Haut Minervois. Close to the town are the remains of a Benedictine abbey, founded in the eighth century, though much of what now remains dates from the eleventh century. The abbey church has a superb Romanesque doorway and a fine Gothic marble altar. The marble is of local origin, the marble quarries here having produced a multi-hued stone that can also be seen in the Royal Palace at Versailles. The town beside the abbey has an array of fine sixteenth- and seventeenth-century houses.

Lagrasse

Close to Caunes is **Rieux-Minervois** where there is an extraordinary church. The church is unique in France, perhaps even in the world, in having seven sides. There is a tradition in southern France for seven sided stars, one that is not well understood despite occasional references to the Seven Pillars of Wisdom of the Proverbs. The church is almost certainly twelfth century, though little is known of its history or builders. The later addition of chapels on the outside walls of the church has obscured that heptagon somewhat, but inside the seven sides are still obvious.

From Rieux head for **Lézignan-Corbières**, a wine town with an interesting museum to the wine producing industry. It is housed in a group of nineteenth-century wine production buildings and includes vineyard, tools and equipment.

South of Lézignan and the A61 **Fabrezan** was the birthplace of Charles Cros, usually credited in French books with having invented the phonograph and colour photography – he was certainly one of the foremost pioneers in each field. A museum has a collection of memorabilia of Cros and exhibitions on his discoveries. Eastwards, at Gasparets the **Musée de la Faune** (Animal Museum) has a collection of stuffed animals and birds from all over the world. The local animals, which include a wild boar and the now almost extinct Pyrenean brown bear are especially interesting.

From Fabrezan it is a short and beautiful journey along the D212 to a stunning view of **Lagrasse**. When, in the late eighth century, Lagrasse stood at the border of the Frankish kingdom and Spain, Charlemagne himself founded a Benedictine monastery here. Later, a village grew up around the abbey, a bridge crossed the river and walls were built to pro-

The Abbaye de Fontfroide

Fontfroide was one of the most important Cistercian abbeys in the south of France. It was founded in 1145, though on the site of an earlier Benedictine house and rapidly became rich and powerful. The abbey was suppressed during the Revolution and fell into disrepair. Then, early this century, it was acquired by a family who, over many decades, have been lovingly restoring it. The original windows have been replaced, some with contemporary stained glass, some with medieval glass rescued from northern churches destroyed during World War I. The abbey church and the thirteenth-century cloisters are superb. In the abbey gardens is a rose garden with over 3,000 variations, the largest collection in the south of France.

History of Narbonne

The Gauls had a town called Narbo here from the sixth century BC onwards, taking advantage of the sheltered inlet of the Mediterranean that is now the Étang de Bages. When the Romans came they made Narbo Martius the capital of Provincia. Later they moved the capital to Lyon, but when they decided to divide Provincia in two they called the regions Narbonensis Prima and Narbonensis Secunda, making Narbonne the capital of Prima. When the Romans departed Narbonne became a Visigoth capital, then a Saracen port and finally a Frankish one.

Under Frankish and Languedoc rule Narbonne became wealthy but then, quite suddenly, the prosperity collapsed in the early fourteenth century; most historians put this down to the expulsion of the city's Jewish merchants and a consequent collapse of commercial acumen. There was an attempt to revive the city's fortunes in the seventeenth century, Pierre-Paul Riquet planning a canal (the Robine) to link his Canal du Midi to Narbonne and the sea. For a variety of reasons this canal took a century to complete by which time Narbonne had – literally – missed the boat.

tect the site. The remains of all of these features can be seen.

The bridge, the seemingly inappropriately named Pont Neuf, is twelfth century. Many of the village houses are fourteenth century: the remnants of the walls date from the same time. The abbey church and abbot's lodging, much of which dates from the thirteenth century, the old (restored) cloisters and new cloisters, built in the eighteenth century, can all be seen. East of Lagrasse is the more impressive **Abbaye de Fontfroide**.

The nearby **Château de Gaussan** was built as a fortified granary/storehouse for the monks, but destroyed at the time of the Revolution. Enthusiasts of the work of Viollet-le-Duc at Carcassonne restored the castle in the nineteenth century.

Places to Visit

Central Aude

Abbaye de Caunes-Minervois

Open: July and August, daily 10am-7pm; April to June, September and October, daily 10am-12noon, 2-6pm; February, March, November and December, Saturday and Sunday 10am-12noon, 2-5pm.
☎ 04 68 78 09 44.

Musée de la Vigne et du Vin

1 Rue Necker, Lézignan-Corbières
Open: All year, daily 9am-7pm.
☎ 04 68 27 07 57.

Musée Charles Cros

Town Hall, Fabrezan
Open: All year Monday-Friday, 9am-12noon, 2-7pm (6pm on Friday).
☎ 04 68 27 81 44.

Musée de la Faune

Gasparets
Open: All year, daily 9.30am-12noon, 2-6pm.
☎ 04 68 27 57 02.

Lagrasse Abbey

Open: May to September, daily 10.30am-12.30pm, 2-6.30pm; October to April, daily 2-5pm.
☎ 04 68 43 15 99 or 04 68 43 10 05.

Abbaye de Fontfroide

Open: July and August, daily 9.30am-6.30pm; September to June, daily 10am-12noon, 2-5pm (4pm from November to March).
☎ 04 68 45 11 08.

Château de Gaussan

Exterior only may be viewed

Musée de la Chapellerie (Hat Museum)

Ginestas
Open: All year Monday-Saturday, 9am-12noon, 2-7pm (6pm from October to May); Sundays, 2.30-8pm (2-6pm May to September).
☎ 04 68 46 19 26.

Musée Archéologique

Peyriac-de-Mer
Open: July and August, 10am-12noon, 5-7pm.
☎ 04 68 42 68 42.

Réserve Africaine (African Reserve)

Nr Sigean
Open: All year, daily 9am-6.30pm (4pm October to May).
☎ 04 68 48 20 20.

NARBONNE

A tour of Narbonne should start at the Canal de la Robine, from where, in summer, boats explore the canal and the *étang* to the south. The canal is crossed by the Pont des Marchands, still covered by the shops the name implies, to reach the huge complex of the cathedral of St Just.

After the Albigensian Crusade, when Narbonne suffered at the hands of the royal army, the French king decided to build a cathedral of such immensity that it would act as symbol of the power of the established church to anyone holding any remaining Cathar sympathies. The proposed cathedral was vast, but when Narbonne's prosperity collapsed the building work stopped, though the visitor finds it

difficult to believe that it was planned to be bigger. What was built is a masterpiece, a magnificent tribute to the medieval stonemason's art. Inside there are fine tombs and polychrome reliefs. Below the Chapel of the Annunciation, the cathedral's treasury houses a collection of reliquaries and old books. There are also two sixteenth-century Flemish tapestries.

Beside the cathedral there is a complex of fine religious buildings. The cloisters are fourteenth-century and beside them is the twelfth-century **Palais Vieux**, the ancient episcopal palace. Between the old palace and the seventeenth century **Palais Neuf** runs the delightful Passage de l'Ancre, while to the west the **Jardin du Musée** is a fine city park.

The museum of the name is, in fact, a pair of museums. **The Musée Archéologique** has many items from Roman Narbonne and the early Christian city, while the **Musée d'Art et d'Histoire** houses the city's art collection. The museum is housed in the beautiful rooms of the archbishop's palace, each of which is named. The Chambre du Roi – in which the Sun King slept on a night in 1642 – has frescoed ceilings and a mosaic floor.

To the north of the cathedral is the **Horreum**, an underground vaulted warehouse of the Roman city. Its mass of small chambers houses a collection of excavated Roman artifacts. Further north, the **Church of St Sébastien**, a fifteenth-century building, is built over the reputed birthplace of the saint whose death by archery is so popular with artists.

From the Horreum or the church, take Rue Droite back to the Place de l'Hôtel de Ville, pausing to admire the fourteenth-century **Tour Martin** and twelfth-century **Donjon Gilles Aycelin** that enclose the façade of the Palais Neuf. The Donjon can be climbed, by way of 179 steps, to a platform that offers a fine view of the city.

South of the canal the chief sight is the **Musée Lapidaire**. Housed in a thirteenth-century, but now deconsecrated church, this museum houses a collection of fragments of stone amassed from the various rebuildings of Narbonne. Another worthwhile site is the **Maison des Trois Nourrices**. The house is sixteenth-century and the name – the House of the Three Wet Nurses – derived from the ample form of the caryatids which support the façade! The name is curious because although three support the main window there are five in total.

Places to Visit

Narbonne

Cathedral Treasury

Open: mid-June to November, daily except Sunday 9.30-11.30am, 2.15-5.30pm; April to mid-June, daily except Sunday 2.30-4.30pm.
☎ 04 68 32 09 52.

Musée Archéologique/ Musée d'Art et d'Histoire

Palais des Archevêques
Open: April to September, daily 9.30am-12.15pm, 2-6pm; October to March, daily except Monday 10am-12noon, 2-5pm.
☎ 04 68 90 30 54 or 04 68 90 30 66.

Horreum

Rue Rouget de l'Isle
Open: April to September, daily 9.30am-12.15pm, 2-6pm; October to March, daily except Monday 10am-12noon, 2-5pm.
☎ 04 68 90 30 54 or 04 68 90 30 66.

Donjon Gilles Aycelin

Open: May to September daily 11am-6pm; October to April daily 10am-12noon, 2-5pm.
☎ 04 68 90 30 13.

Musée Lapidaire

Eglise Notre-Dame de Lamourguier, Boulevard Ferroul
Open: July and August, daily 9.30am-12.15pm, 2-6pm.
☎ 04 68 90 30 54 or 04 68 90 30 66.

AROUND NARBONNE

To the north of Narbonne there is pleasant country, though with little to detain the visitor. Of the more interesting little places one is Ginestas, a wine village with a fine church and a museum of hats from all over the world.

To the east of Narbonne the limestone ridge of the **Montagne de la Clape** separates the city from the sea: the summit of the ridge (at 702ft – 214m) can be reached by walks of about an hour from either its western or north-eastern edges and offers a superb view.

East of the ridge is **Narbonne-Plage**, a modern resort with an excellent beach. To the north, follow the D1118, park as signed and take the path for a walk of about 10 minutes to the **Gouffre de l'Oeil Doux**.

The Cave of the Sweet Eye, standing about $1/2$ mile (less than 1km) from the sea, has a pool of pure water. This oddity has created the legend that the pool is of supernatural origin and it is claimed to be bottomless. Far more fathomable is the small *étang* to the north. Close to this the Aude reaches the sea, but it is not for that memorable event that the *étang* is named. This is the **Étang de Pissvaches**, which translates exactly as you thought it might.

South of Narbonne-Plage the road reaches **Gruissan**, a village set on an island in the salt lagoons south of the Montagne de la Clape. Gruissan was once an outlying part of Narbonne, but is now a small fishing port connected to the sea by a canal, together with a small marina and resort. The town's houses are in a series on concentric rings around the ruins of a thirteenth-century tower known as **Tour Barbarousse**. The Barbarossa (Red Beard) of the name is not known with certainty but is more likely to have been a sixteenth-century Turkish mercenary than the twelfth-century German emperor.

From Gruissan the visitor must return to Narbonne in order to explore the coast to the south, there being neither road nor walking to **Port-la-Nouvelle** because of **the Grau de la Vieille Nouvelle**, the narrow mouth of the **Étang de l'Ayrolle**. From Narbonne, the first place reached is **Peyriac-de-Mer** where a small museum has items excavated from local prehistoric, Gallic and Roman sites.

Nearby, the **African Reserve** is a drive-through safari park with not only the standard animals such as lions, but white rhinoceros and Tibetan bears. There is also a walk-through park with zebra, camels etc. On the *étang* that forms part of the park there are pelicans, flamingoes and other birds.

To the south, the road leads to the **Étang de Lapalme** before reaching **Leucate-Plage**, another good beach resort. **Port-Leucate**, the last place on the coast before Roussillon, is another port quietly turning itself into a resort. Here the emphasis is on water-sports on the **Étang de Leucate**. On the far side of the *étang* is **Fitou**, a pretty little village whose name appears on the label of one of the best of Languedoc wines.

SOUTH OF CARCASSONNE

Here the D118 follows the Aude, the river defining the western edge of the Corbières. But first go west to visit Montréal and Fanjeaux.

Detail of fountain, Limoux centre

Montréal and Fanjeaux

Montréal derives its name from Mont Royal, the same root as that for the city in Canada. Here, legend has it, the meeting took place between the Bishop of Toulouse, a Cathar sympathizer, and Dominic de Guzman, a local Catholic who was later sanctified. Dominic had written his beliefs on a sheet of paper that the Bishop's followers stole and attempted to burn. The paper refused to ignite which the Catholics used to justify their pursuance of the Cathars. Within the village the lovely fourteenth-century, Gothic church has a fine eighteenth-century organ on which regular recitals are given in the summer months.

At **Fanjeaux** – the curious name derives from Fanum Jovis, Temple of Jupiter – is St Dominic's house, decorated with a stained glass window that portrays the several miracles, besides the one mentioned in Montréal, that the saint performed in his mission against the Cathars. A monastery founded by St Dominic stands in the hamlet of **Prouille**, close to Fanjeaux on the road to Montréal. The church is worth visiting for the chapel of St Dominic (and another representation of the miracle of the fire) and a small treasury which includes several interesting medieval reliquaries.

On the D118 the first major place of interest is **Limoux**, a pleasant town with a fourteenth-century Pont Neuf (!), a fine church and some delightful fifteenth- and sixteenth-century houses.

Close to Limoux, the chapel of **Notre-Dame de Marceille** is de-

Le Blanquette de Limoux

Le Blanquette de Limoux is the town's famous sparkling wine, claimed to be the oldest in the world. It is first mentioned in a document of 1531, a great deal earlier than can be claimed by Champagne with which Le Blanquette has often (and invariably to its detriment) been compared. The comparison is unfair, the two not being quite the same and Champagne having an appeal (a snobbery appeal for want of a better way of expressing it) that means that real comparisons are almost impossible.

lightfully positioned and famous for its Black Virgin, a statue dating from the eleventh century and still attracting pilgrims and votive offerings. **St Hilaire** has an abbey, which was founded in the eighth century for Benedictine monks (who are credited by several reputable authorities with having invented the sparkling La Blanquette). The abbey was dissolved in 1748. The abbey church dates from the twelfth century and houses, in the chapel on the right, the sarcophagus of St Sernin, founder of the first church in Toulouse in the 3rd century. Scenes from the life of the saint are carved on three faces. Beside the church are the abbey's fourteenth-century cloisters, an elegant square in Gothic style.

There is another abbey at **St Polycarpe**. Though it is less well preserved than St Hilaire it is interesting for the church having been fortified, for its sculpted Carolingian altar and some scraps of fourteenth-century frescoes. There is yet another abbey at **Alet-les-Bains**, a beautiful little village – a spa since Roman times – that still preserves an array of fine medieval houses. Despite its size, the village was important to the religious community: a Benedictine abbey was built here in the eleventh century, its church becoming a cathedral when Pope John XXII made it a bishopric in 1318. The cathedral was wrecked by Huguenots in 1577, but is still impressive.

Shoes and hats

Beyond Alet is **Couiza**, a shoe-making town with a fine sixteenth-century castle. To the west, **Espéraza** was known for hat-making and has a museum to the trade and another to dinosaur fossils, some unearthed locally. **Quillan**, the next town, is also a focus for shoe-making. It is pleasantly set on the Aude, but is more a base for explorations to the south and west than visited in its own right.

To the south-west lies the **Plateau de Sault**, a forested plateau that sits above 3,280ft (1,000m). The plateau is crossed by the D613 towards **Montaillou** (in Ariège), which has achieved international fame as a result of the French historian Emmanuel le Roy Ladurie's book on it.

From Quillan the D117 reaches **Puivert**. The château here was originally built in the twelfth century but was destroyed by Simon de Montfort in 1210 after it had been occupied by Cathars. The castle was rebuilt in the fourteenth century and includes a fine keep and an impressively large courtyard. Within the keep there are eight sculptures of medieval musicians. These have been used as the basis of constructing replica instruments that are displayed in the **Musée de la Quercorb**. The museum's name derives from that given to the country to the north-west of Quillan, a secret landscape of few roads. The museum also explores the Quercorb's traditions and history.

To the north of **Puivert Chalabre** is a pretty village of quaint stone houses. The **Château de Caudeval**, near the village, was held by Cathars, falling in 1209, and was besieged again in 1575, this time by Huguenots.

From Quillan the D117 goes south through the **Défilé de Pierre-Lys** where the cliffs hug the Aude so tight that the road builders had to dig short tunnels and carve out rock overhangs to get the road through. On each side there are huge spires and crags of white limestone. **Axat** is a base for river rafting on the infant Aude, while a right turn leads to the **Château de Puilarens**, an impressively positioned tenth-century castle, though enlarged later when it stood on the border with Catalonia.

On the D118 beyond Axat, the **Gorges de St Georges** is almost as exciting as the earlier *défilé*, but then the country opens out, the Aude running in a beautiful, broad and deeply wooded valley. The road runs along the Ariège border for a while, finally entering Pyrénées-Orientales near **Puyvalador**, from where, even in summer, there are glimpses of snow on the high Pyrenean peaks.

From Couiza a tortuous road rises to Rennes-le-Château. This curious village was once a local capital, with a population measured in thousands, when it was destroyed by the army of the King of Aragon in 1170. But the real interest here is the story of the village's priest, the Abbé Berengar Saunière who served from 1890 until his death in 1919, except for one short period around 1896.

The problem that led to his suspension was the spending of large sums of money on himself and on beautifying his church. Saunière was not a rich man and a village priest's salary was tiny – where did it all come from? Asked by his bishop, Saunière refused to tell, was suspended, but re-instated after an appeal to Rome. He never did say where the cash came from and died penniless.

At the time, and since, the speculation has been rife. He is said to have discovered the treasure of the Knights Templar, or the Visigoths, or the Cathars. He is said to have discovered evidence that Jesus and Mary Magdalene escaped Jerusalem after the Crucifixion and set up home in the Corbières, founding the Merovingian dynasty. It is said that the priest who heard his last confession was so shocked by what he heard that he refused to return to the dying man, leaving him on his own to die, five days later, without having received the last rites. Saunière is said to have carved 'This Place is Terrible' above the door of the church.

The story has spawned dozens of books and even more theories. Tales of treasure have necessitated the erection of 'No Digging' signs, and some villagers have cashed in on a supposed black magic connection. All in all it is an intriguing place. There is a small museum to Saunière in the church's presbytery and another in his old house, but the collections and memorabilia shed virtually no light on the episode.

Musée

Open: All year, daily 10am-7pm (6pm October to April).
☎ 04 68 74 72 68.

Domaine de l'Abbé Saunière

Open: All year, daily 10am-7pm.
☎ 04 68 74 31 16.

LES CORBIERÈS

The country of Les Corbierès, sandwiched between the Pyrenean foothills and the valley taken by the Aude and the Canal du Midi, is a wonderful land of rock outcrops, scrub and vineyards. It is sparsely populated, yet has one of the densest collections of abbeys and castles in France. The castles are easily explained: this was once frontier country, a land on the border of France and Spain. The abbeys reflect a frontier world too, one where, at first, the church represented a spiritual escape from the harshness of life in a country where the summers burnt the land and the winters froze it.

Château de Peyrepertuse

Later, the church represented the establishment against the rise of heresies that implied the locals might be trying to think for themselves. Today Corbières is famous for its wines which many argue are the best that Languedoc has to offer, and for some of the most dramatic and picturesque ruins in France.

Château de Quéribus near Cucugnan is reached by a steep, narrow road to a car park from where an even steeper path (allow 20 minutes for the climb up) ascends. An earlier castle was the last stronghold of the Cathars, falling only in 1255. The castle was immediately strengthened, acting as a frontier bastion with Catalonia until Roussillon joined France. The view from the castle – both towards the Pyrenees (particularly Le Canigou) and the Corbières, is as good as it is expansive.

From Quéribus those with sharp eyes will see the best of all the Corbières castles, **Peyrepertuse**, on a rocky pinnacle to the west of **Cucugnan**. Legend has it that Charlemagne built the first castle on the pinnacles now occupied by the Château de Peyrepertuse, though the first known fortress dates from the tenth century. The Cathars held out here, but though virtually impregnable, the castle was also difficult to keep supplied without support and was surrendered. The French then extended the lower castle (Château Bas) – the first buildings reached by the path – and added the higher buildings (the Château St Georges).

The castle is an engineering mar-

Rafting on the River Aude

vel, to such an extent that how anyone even came up with the idea beggars belief. The limestone pinnacles on which it stands are tall and sheer and the buildings extend 900ft (275m) along the narrow tops. Between the high and low buildings the 'Esplanade Ouest' is a wider area, but at the prow of each of the castles the drops are impressive. Just thinking about how the walls at the edge were constructed will make the visitor's hair stand on end.

Remarkably, many of the drops are unprotected: please be careful, especially if you have children, the castle is built into the rock so that in places the ground slopes in two directions at once and is polished. For safety reasons the castle is closed if winds are high or rain heavy.

• THE CASTLES OF LES CORBIÈRES •

East of Couiza is the **Château d'Arques**. This rectangle with corner turrets and a square keep, is late thirteenth-century, but there may have been an earlier building as Cathar parfaits are known to have stayed in the area from the end of the twelfth century.

Château d'Arques: Open: July and August, daily 10am-7pm; May, June and September, daily 10am-6pm; October and April, daily 10am-5pm.
☎ 04 68 69 82 87 or 04 68 69 84 77.

From Peyrepertuse – a village whose name is almost as big as itself – the D212 to Auriac goes through Corbières at its best – beautiful wooded country with occasional excellent long views and then the sudden appearance of a castle. **Château d'Auriac**, built at the edge of an old copper-mining village, is perched on the edge of a sheer cliff.

Château d'Auriac: Open: Any reasonable time.

East of Auriac, over the Col de Bedos, are **Château de Termes** and **Château de Durfort**. A visit to the former requires a 15 minute walk, but is worthwhile as the ruins are romantically set, close to the **Gorges de Terminet**. This castle was another Cathar stronghold, surrendered to Simon de Montfort when the occupiers were decimated by dysentery after a four-month siege. Durfort was also taken by de Montfort. It has withstood the test of time less well, but is not open to visitors.

Château de Termes: Open: July and August, daily 9.30am-7.30pm; May, June and September, daily 10am-6pm; April and October, daily 10am-5pm; November and March Saturday and Sunday 10am-5pm.
☎ 04 68 70 09 20.

Villerouge-Termenes, a village of ancient houses, is also dominated by a castle, one that was surrendered to Simon de Montfort at the same time as that at Termes. The rectangular castle has semi-circular towers at each corner, one of these having acted as the keep. In summer the castle is used for spectacles that re-create medieval Languedocian life.

Château de Villerouge-Termenes: Open: July and August, daily 9am-8pm; May, June and September, daily 10am-6pm; April and October, daily 10am-5pm.
☎ 04 68 70 09 11.

At nearby **Durban-Corbières**, once a fortified village, the castle includes a delightful courtyard flanked by towers.

Château de Durban-Corbierès: Open: July and August, daily 10am-12noon, 3-7pm. ☎ 04 68 45 94 85.

Finally, cross the **Col d'Extrême** to reach the **Château d'Aguilar**, an impressive ruin that saw action not only during the Albigensian Crusade but also during several centuries of border skirmishing between the French and the Spanish.

Château d'Aguilar
Open: All year, daily 10am-5pm ☎ 04 68 45 51 00

South of Carcassonne

Abbaye de St Hilaire

Nr Limoux
Open: July to September,
daily 9am-7pm.
☎ 04 68 69 41 15 for information.

Abbaye de St Polycarpe

Nr Limoux
Open: May to September,
daily 8am-7pm; October to April,
daily 9am-5pm.
☎ 04 68 31 14 31.

Ruined Cathedral

Alet-les-Bains
Open: April to mid-September,
daily 9am-12noon, 2-6.30pm;
mid-September to March,
daily 9am-12noon, 3-5pm.
☎ 04 68 69 93 56.

Musée de la Chapellerie

Espéraza
Open: July and August, daily 10am-
7pm, September to June, Monday-
Friday 10am-12noon, 2-6pm.
☎ 04 68 74 00 75.

Musée des Dinosaures

Espéraza
Open: July and August, daily 10am-
7pm, September to June, Monday-
Friday 10am-12noon, 2-6pm.
☎ 04 68 74 26 88.

Château de Puivert

Open: April to October, daily 8am-
8pm; November to March,
daily 10am-4pm.
☎ 04 68 20 81 52.

Musée de la Quercorb

Puivert
Open: July and August, daily 10am-
7pm, April to June and September,
daily 10am-12noon, 2-6pm, October
to March, Saturday and Sunday 10am
12noon, 2-5pm.
☎ 04 68 20 80 98.

Château de Puilarens

Open: July and August, daily 9am-
8pm; April to June and September,
daily 10am-6pm; October, daily
10am-5pm.
☎ 04 68 20 65 26.

Château de Quéribus

Open: July and August, daily 9am-
8pm; May, June and September, daily
10am-7pm; October to December and
February to April, daily 10am-6pm.
☎ 04 68 45 03 69.

Château de Peyrepertuse

Open: July and August, daily 9am-
8pm; April to June and September,
daily 10am-7pm; November to March,
daily 10am-6pm.
☎ 04 68 45 03 26.

Château de Quéribus

GETTING THERE

By Air

Montpellier and Toulouse are served by many international airlines. Air Inter, the French domestic carrier, also operates flights from Paris to Toulouse and Montpellier as well as other, smaller, airports.

By Rail

SNCF (Systéme Nationale de Chemin-de-Fer), the French national railway company, has both fast and express trains linking Paris with other parts of France and the Channel ports. Of particular interest for the traveller keen to cut down on travel time is the TGV (pronounced Tay-Jay-Vay) service, a very fast 155mph (250kph) bullet-shaped train that speeds between Paris and the South. The TGV offers only first class accommodation but does cut journey time considerably.

SNCF also offer motorail services to those not wishing to spend a part of their holiday gazing at a ribbon of Autoroute. These services are available for the Channel ports and Paris. The service is not cheap, but the journey is overnight, which does have the advantage of extending the holiday by a day if travelling is not considered to be part of the holiday. Night-time accommodation is in a couchette – six berths, in three tiers, to a compartment, with blanket and pillow supplied – or in T1, T2 or T3 cabins. As the names imply, these offer one (first class ticket only), two or three berths. Breakfast at the destination is included in the price of the ticket.

By Road

Car

The north-eastern tip of the area covered by this book is served by the A7, the Autoroute du Soleil. At Orange the A9 splits off, traversing the whole of southern Languedoc to reach the Spanish border. Carcassonne is reached by the A61 from Toulouse, which links to the A7 near Narbonne. The A75 will eventually link Clermont-Ferrand to Béziers and Montpellier , but is, at present, not complete. The recent decision to build a vast bridge over the Tarn Gorge and Larzac Plateau near Millau to carry this bridge was taken after a prolonged campaign by conservationists and has not been greeted with universal acclaim. All French autoroutes are toll roads. There are rest areas approximately every $12^1/_2$ miles (20km) and service areas approximately every 25 miles (40km). The area is also served by an excellent system of good quality 'ordinary' roads.

Coaches and Buses

France has an extensive, long-distance coach system and good local bus services. Not surprisingly, the majority of long-distance coach services head for Paris.

WHEN YOU ARE THERE

Accommodation

Languedoc has accommodation ranging from luxurious hotels to small camp sites, and everything in between. All the local Tourist Offices have brochures on hotels and camping sites in their area. The French Government Tourist Office in your home country will also be able to supply information on hotels.

Gîtes de France offers furnished accommodation for self-catering. For details contact:

Gîtes de France
59 Rue St-Lazare
75439 Paris Cedex 09
☎ 01 49 70 75 75.

The French Youth Hostel Association can be contacted at:

Lique Française pour les Auberges de la Jeunesse
38 Boulevard Raspail
75007 Paris
☎ 01 45 48 69 84.
www.fuaj.fr

Car Travel

Car hire is available from many companies, including all the well-known major European ones, and from all the big towns, the airports and all large railway stations.

The speed limits currently applied to French roads are:

	In dry conditions	In the wet
Autoroutes	81mph (130kph)	68mph (110kph)
National roads	68mph (110kph)	62mph (100kph)
Other roads	56mph (90kph)	50mph (80kph)
In towns	31mph (50kph)	31mph (50kph)

Please note:
There are new speed limits on autoroutes: a minimum of 50mph (80kph) for the outside lane during daylight, on level ground and with good visibility; and a maximum of 31mph (50kph) if the visibility is less than 55yd (50m).

No driving is permitted on a provisional licence and the minimum age to drive is 18. Stop signs mean exactly that – the vehicle must come to a complete halt.

It is compulsory for front seat passengers to wear seat belts and children below the age of 10 are not allowed to travel in the front seats. All vehicles must carry a red warning triangle and a spare headlamp bulb.

There are strict – and very strictly interpreted – laws on speeding and drink-driving. The former will usually result in an on-the-spot fine, while the latter will usually result in confiscation of the car.

In built-up areas, the motorist must usually give way to anybody coming out of a side-turning on the right. This is indicated by the sign, priorité à droite. However, this rule no longer applies at roundabouts which means vehicles already on the roundabout have right of way (passage protégé). All roads of any significance outside built-up areas have right of way.

Car Parking

Car parking is no easier in French towns than it is in most other large European cities. The by-laws vary from town to town and, occasionally, from day to day. To be safe it is best to use car parks. Check before leaving your parked car: it is common practice to take your ticket with you, to pay as you return and to use the stamped ticket or token to raise the exit barrier. If you drive to an exit and then discover this rule, it is likely that you will have a queue of cars behind you when you are trying to work out what has gone wrong or are trying to reverse. Since tokens are time-limited, the queue is unlikely to be sympathetic.

Currency Regulations

The French unit of currency is the French franc. There are no restrictions on the import of French or foreign currency but amounts must be declared if bank notes worth in excess of 5,000 French francs are likely to be exported.

Customs Regulations and Entry into France

Normal EEC customs regulations apply for those travelling from Britain. Normal European regulations apply for those travelling from North America.

No visa is required for holders of British, American and Canadian passports.

Disabled Visitors

Not all the sites listed in this guide are accessible to disabled visitors. A list of those that are, not only in Lnaguedoc but in the whole of France, can be found in the publication *Touristes quand même! Promenades en France pour les voyageurs handicapés*. This excellent guide can be obtained from:

Comité National Français de Liaison
pour la Réadaptiondes Handicapés
38 Boulevard Raspail
75007 Paris

The guide will be of interest not only to those with a physical handicap, but to the visually handicapped and visitors with a hearing difficulty.

Fact File

Electricity

220v AC, 50 Hertz (cycles/sec) in most places. Some small areas are still at 110v AC. Adapters will be needed by those people who do not use continental two-pin plugs at home.

Finances

All major credit cards (Access, Visa, American Express etc) are taken at most large restaurants, hotels, shops and garages. Eurocheques and travellers' cheques are also accepted.

Banks are normally open from 9am-12noon, 2-4.30pm, Monday to Friday only. They close early on the day before a Bank Holiday.

Health Care

British travellers have a right to claim health services in France by virtue of EEC regulations. Form E111 – available from the Department of Health and Social Security – should be obtained to avoid complications.

American and Canadian visitors will need to check the validity of their personal health insurance to guarantee they are adequately covered. For emergency assistance, dial 19 in all towns. In country areas it may be necessary to phone the local *gendarmerie* (police).

Pharmacies, clearly marked with a green cross, can usually deal with minor ailments or advise people where to go if any additional help is needed.

Holidays

France has the following national holidays:

New Year's Day
Easter Monday
May Day
Ascension Day
VE Day – 8 May
Whit Monday
Bastille Day – 14 July
Assumption Day – 15 August
All Saints' Day – 1 November
Armistice Day – 11 November
Christmas Day

Measurements

France uses the metric system. Conversions are:

1 kilogram (1,000 grams) = 2.2lb
1 litre = 1 3/4 pints
4.5 litres = 1 gallon
1.6 km = 1 mile
1 hectare = 2 1/2 acres (approx)

La Malène

*Above; Left: **Tarn Gorge** Right: **St Guilhem-le-Désert***
*Below: **Place de la Liberté, St Guilhem-le-Désert***

Fact File

Post and Telephone Services

Stamps (*timbres*) are available from post offices, which are normally open from 8am-7pm Monday to Friday and 8am-12noon on Saturday. In some smaller towns and villages, the post office may be shut for lunch, both the timing and the duration of the break being a local custom.

Telephones in France take coins rather than tokens. The dial codes from France are:

Great Britain	19 44
Canada	19 1
USA	19 1

Remember to leave out the first zero of your home country number – eg to dial the French Government Tourist Office in London (071 491 7622) from France, dial 19 44 17 491 7622. Many telephone booths now take phonecards; buy the *télécarte* from post offices and where advertised on telephone booths. Calls can be received at phone boxes where the blue bell is shown.

Within France, remember that a new code system has recently been introduced. This divides the country into five regions and gives them an additional two-digit number. Thus all numbers in France now have 10 digits. Southern France, including Languedoc, is 04. Thus to dial a number in Montpellier it is now necessary to dial (within France) 04 followed by the 8 digit code. When dialling from the UK the first 0 must be dropped (ie. 00 33 4 xx xx xx xx).

Sports

Languedoc is an ideal area for the sportsman. The coast and the inland *étangs* and lakes offer endless opportunities for the sailor, with many of the resorts priding themselves on the quality of their facilities and the local winds.

The upland areas are ideal for the walker, with numerous GRs (Grande Randonnée) crossing the region, particularly in the Cévennes National Park. For information on the entire GR system, contact:

Fédération Française de la Randonnée Pedestre
Comité de Promotion des Sentiers de Grande Randonnée
64 Rue de Gergovie
75014 Paris
☎ 01 45 45 31 02.

The area is also of interest to the horse rider. For information on the French system of equestrian paths contact:

Délégation Nationale de Tourisme Équestre
30 Avenue d'Iéna
75116 Paris
☎ 01 53 67 44 44.

Not surprisingly Languedoc had a great caving tradition. Most visitors will settle for the show caves, but those who wish to explore other systems should contact:

Fédération Française de Spéléologie
130 Rue St-Maur
75011 Paris
☎ 01 43 57 56 54.

The rivers of Languedoc are excellent for canoeing and rafting and many riverside towns and villages offer canoe hire or rafting trips. Ask at the local Tourist Information Office for details.

Golf is becoming increasingly popular in France and Languedoc-Roussillon has some very good courses. The local Tourist Information Office will let you have details or you can contact the national organisation:

Fédération Française de Golf
69 Avenue Victor Hugo
75783 Paris Cedex 16
☎ 01 44 17 63 00.

In winter, the upland areas around the Cévennes National Park are snow-covered, offering great sport for the cross-country skier, but fewer opportunities for the downhill enthusiast. Contact:

Comité Régional de Ski des Cévennes
Espace République
20 Rue de la République
34000 Montpellier
☎ 04 67 22 94 92.

Tipping

Tips (*pourboires*) are given as in your home country but in France they also apply to guides at both châteaux and museums.

Tourist Offices in France

Almost all towns and many villages have their own Syndicats d'Initiative and these will supply local information and maps.

The main offices for the *départements* of Languedoc are listed below.

Comité Régional du Tourisme Languedoc-Roussillon
20 Rue de la République
34000 Montpellier
☎ 04 67 22 81 00

Fax: 04 67 58 06 10
www.cr-languedocroussillon.fr/tourisme

Continued on page 136...

Above: *Cirque du Moureze*

Left: *Transhumance*

Above; Left: *Aigues-Mortes* Right: *Uzés*
Below: *GR signs, summit of Mont Aigoual*

Comité National des Sentiers de Grande Randonnée
Ici se croisent les principaux GR créés dans les
Cévennes par le Dr Cabouat, inaugurés en 1962
le GR Alpes Pyrénées, le
GR7 sentier Paul Arnaud Vosges Pyrénées,
le GR66 Tour de l'Aigoual

✕Aire de Cote 2h ⌂ ⌂Barre des Cévennes 8h30	GR 7.66	GR 7.66	Col de la Cereirède 1h15 → l'Espérou 1h 45 ⌂
✕Aire de Cote 2h ⌂ ✕Colognac 10h ⌂	GR 6	GR 6	la Croix de Fer 2h15 🚌 Meyrueis 4h 45 ⌂
GR 6A	Col de Prat-Peirot 45' Meyrueis 4h30 ⌂ 🚌	GR 6B	Col del Bes 1h 45 Meyrueis 4h 45 ⌂

Comité Départemental du Tourisme de l'Aude
Centre Administratif Départemental
11855 Carcassonne Cedex 09
☎ 04 68 11 66 00

Comité Départemental du Tourisme du Gard
3 Place des Arénes – BP 122
30010 Nîmes Cedex
☎ 04 66 21 02 51

Comité Départemental du Tourisme de l'Hérault
Avenue des Moulins – BP 3067
34034 Montpellier Cedex 1
☎ 04 67 67 71 71
www.cdt-herault.fr

Comité Départemental du Tourisme de la Lozère
14 Boulevard Henri Bourillon – BP4
48001 Mende Cedex
☎ 04 66 65 60 00

Website for all French regions:
www.franceguide.com/gb/regions

Tourist Offices outside France
(French Government)

Great Britain
178 Piccadily
London W1V 0AL
☎ 071 493 6594
www.franceguide.com

United States of America
444 Madison Avenue
New York
NY 10022
☎ 212 838 7800
www.francetourism.com

676 North Michigan Avenue
Suite 3360
Chicago
IL60611-2819
☎ 312 751 7800

9454 Wilshire Boulevard
Suite 715
Beverley Hills
CA 90212-2967
☎ 310 271 2693

Canada
30 St Patrick's Street
Suite 700
Toronto ONT
M5T 3A3
☎ 416 593 4723

1981 Avenue McGill College
Tour Esso Suite 490
Montreal PQ
Quebec
H3A 2 W9
☎ 514 288 4264

Useful Addresses
Consulates-General
Great Britain
24 Avenue du Prado
Marseille
☎ 04 91 53 43 32

United States of America
9 Rue Armeny
Marseille
☎ 04 91 54 92 00

Canada
24 Avenue du Prado
Marseille
☎ 04 91 37 19 37/37 19 40

Weather Information

	Temperature (Max) (°C)	Rainfall (Max) (cm)
January	12.4	7.8
February	11.5	8.1
March	12.5	5.7
April	17.6	5.8
May	20.1	5.0
June	26.5	3.7
July	28.4	2.4
August	28.1	3.9
September	26.1	8.0
October	21.1	12.2
November	15.8	6.9
December	13.5	6.5

These data are for Montpellier, but will apply all along the coast and on the inland plain. In winter the temperatures will be much lower in upland Languedoc.

LANDMARK
VISITORS GUIDES

US & British Virgin Islands

US & British VI*
ISBN: 1 901522 03 2
256pp,
UK £11.95 US $15.95

Antigua & Barbuda

Antigua & Barbuda*
ISBN: 1 901522 02 4
96pp,
UK £5.95 US $12.95

Bermuda

Bermuda*
ISBN: 1 901522 07 5
160pp,
UK £7.95 US $12.95

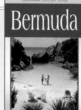

Barbados

Barbados*
ISBN: 1 901522 32 6
160pp,
UK £7.95 US $12.95

St Lucia

St Lucia*
ISBN: 1 901522 82 2
144pp,
UK £6.95 US $13.95

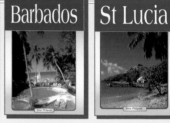
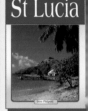

Cayman Islands

Cayman Islands*
ISBN: 1 901522 33 4
160pp
UK £7.95 US $12.95

Jamaica

Jamaica*
ISBN: 1 901522 31 8
160pp
UK £7.95 US $12.95

Orlando & Central Florida

Orlando*
ISBN: 1 901522 22 9
256pp,
UK £9.95 US $15.95

Florida: Gulf Coast

Florida: Gulf Coast*
ISBN: 1 901522 01 6
160pp
UK £7.95 US $12.95

Florida: The Keys

Florida: The Keys*
ISBN: 1 901522 21 0
160pp,
UK £7.95 US $12.95

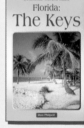

Dominican Republic

Dominican Republic*
ISBN: 1 901522 08 3
160pp,
UK £7.95 US $12.95

Gran Canaria

Gran Canaria*
ISBN: 1 901522 19 9
160pp
UK £7.95 US $12.95

Tenerife

Tenerife
ISBN: 1 901522 17 2
160pp,
UK £7.95

Northern Cyprus

North Cyprus
ISBN: 1 901522 51 2
192pp
UK £8.95

Madeira

Madeira
ISBN: 1 901522 42
192pp,
UK £8.95

Provence*
ISBN: 1 901522 45 8
240pp,
UK £10.95 US $17.95

Côte d'Azur*
ISBN: 1 901522 29 6
144pp,
UK £6.95 US $13.95

Dordogne
ISBN: 1 901522 67 9
224pp,
UK £11.95

Vendée
ISBN: 1 901522 76 X
96pp,
UK £4.95

Pack
2 months
into
2 weeks
with your
Landmark
Visitors
Guides

Bruges*
ISBN: 1 901522 66 0
96pp,
UK £5.95

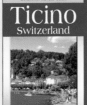

Ticino
ISBN: 1 901522 74 1
192pp
UK £8.95

Italian Lakes*
ISBN: 1 901522 11 3
240pp,
UK £10.95 US $15.95

Riga*
ISBN: 1 901522 59 8
160pp,
UK £7.95

Cracow
ISBN: 1 901522 54 7
160pp,
UK £7.95

New Zealand*
ISBN: 1 901522 36 9
320pp
UK £12.95 US $18.95

Iceland*
ISBN: 1 901522 68 7
192pp,
UK £12.95 US $17.95

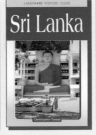

Sri Lanka
ISBN: 1 901522 37 7
192pp,
UK £9.95

India: Kerala
ISBN: 1 901522 16 4
256pp,
UK £10.99

India: Goa
ISBN: 1 901522 23 7
160pp,
UK £7.95

Prices subject to alteration from time to time

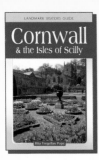

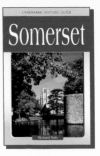

Cornwall
ISBN: 1 901522 09 1
256pp, Full colour
£9.95

Devon
ISBN: 1 901522 42 3
224pp, Full colour
£9.95

Dorset
ISBN: 1 901522 46 6
240pp, Full colour
£9.95

Somerset
ISBN: 1 901522 40 7
224pp, Full colour
£10.95

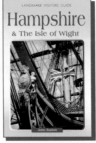

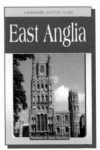

Cotswolds
ISBN: 1 901522 12 1
224pp, Full colour
£9.99

Hampshire
ISBN: 1 901522 14 8
224pp, Full colour
£9.95

East Anglia
ISBN: 1 901522 58 X
224pp, Full colour
£9.95

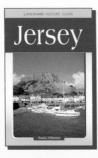

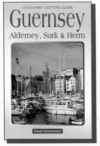

Scotland
ISBN: 1 901522 18 0
288pp, Full colour
£11.95

Jersey
ISBN: 1 901522 47 4
224pp, Full colour
£9.99

Guernsey
ISBN: 1 901522 48 2
224pp, Full colour
£9.95

Harrogate
ISBN: 1 901522 55 5
96pp, Full colour
£4.95

VISITORS GUIDES
TO THE UK

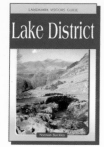

Lake District
ISBN: 1 901522 38 5
224pp, Full colour
£9.95

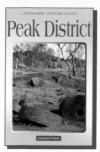

Peak District
ISBN: 1 901522 25 3
240pp, Full colour
£9.99

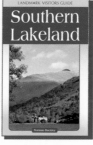

Southern Lakeland
ISBN: 1 901522 53 9
96pp, Full colour
£5.95

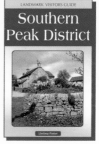

Southern Peak
ISBN: 1 901522 27 X
96pp, Full colour
£5.95

West Cornwall
ISBN: 1 901522 24 5
96pp, Full colour
£5.95

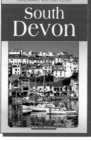

South Devon
ISBN: 1 901522 52 0
96pp, Full colour
£5.95

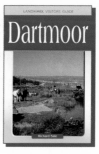

Dartmoor
ISBN: 1 901522 69 5
96pp, Full colour
£5.95

New Forest
ISBN: 1 901522 70 9
96pp, Full colour
£5.95

Isle of Wight
ISBN: 1 901522 71 7
96pp, Full colour
£5.95

Yorkshire Dales
ISBN: 1 901522 41 5
224pp, Full colour
£9.95

Pack
2 months
into
2 weeks
with your
Landmark
Visitors
Guides

For ordering details, see page 139

Published by
Landmark Publishing Ltd,
Waterloo House, 12 Compton, Ashbourne, Derbyshire DE6 1DA England
Tel: (01335) 347349 Fax: (01335) 347303 e-mail: landmark@clara.net
web site: www.landmarkpublishing.co.uk

1st Edition
ISBN 1 901 522 79 2

British Library Cataloguing in Publication Data: a catalogue record for this book is
available from the British Library.

Print: Gutenberg Press Ltd, Malta
Design & Cartography: James Allsopp
Editor: Kay Coulson
Proof reader: Tim Rose

Front cover: St Chely-du-Tarn
Back cover, top: Place de la Camédie, Montpellier
Back cover, bottom: La Malene

Picture Credits:
All photographs are supplied by the author.